MW00607068

THE
UNLUCKY
SPERM CLUB

Byrdylynn
Always Trust in your
own wings!
Best of Luck in All
That yw DO!
Nelson Head

THE
UNLUCKY
SPERM CLUB

YOU ARE NOT A VICTIM OF YOUR CIRCUMSTANCES
BUT A PRODUCT OF YOUR CHOICES

NELSON TRESSLER

t48
PUBLISHING

Copyright © 2020 Nelson L. Tressler

All rights reserved. No part of this publication may be reproduced, distributed, or transmitted in any form or by any means, including photocopying, recording, or other electronic or mechanical methods, without the prior written permission of the publisher, except in the case of brief quotations embodied in critical reviews and certain other noncommercial uses permitted by copyright law. For permission requests, write to the publisher, PO Box 750441 Las Vegas, NV 89136 "Attention: Permissions Coordinator," at the address below.

T48 Publishing
PO Box 750441
Las Vegas, NV 89136
T48publishing@6m2s.com

ISBN: 978-1-7355014-2-0 (hardcover)
ISBN: 978-1-7355014-0-6 (paperback)
ISBN: 978-1-7355014-1-3 (ebook)
ISBN: 978-1-7355014-3-7 (audiobook)

Ordering Information:
Special discounts are available on quantity purchases by corporations, associations, and others. For details, contact PO Box 750441 Las Vegas, NV 89136 or email at T48publishing@6m2s.com.

Dedication

To the three women who helped me get to where I am today, my gram, Gloria Tressler, my mom, Diane Burns, my wife, Skye Tressler, and to the three young men who motivate me to continue on my journey to help make this world a better place, my sons, Dawson, Branson, and Grayson. I love you all.

Acknowledgments

First, I would like to thank my loving Heavenly Father and my Savior Jesus Christ.

I would like to thank my family in Pennsylvania. I know that the publishing of this book is going to bring new interest to horrible events that you are all trying to forget. I, too, felt the same way, wanting to never have to answer another question about what my grandfather did and how I fit in to the scenario. I pray that you all will understand why I must write this book. I realize that it may feel like I'm opening up old wounds, however, it is actually my way of attempting to heal my own wounds by talking about it and coming to the reality that I had no control over the situation, and that I am not going to be defined by either the actions or the opinions of others. As soon as I started to realize that I had the power to assign whatever meaning I wanted to, to what Pap did and what it meant for me and my life, was when I quit being ashamed by what happened and started to gather strength from the events that caused me so much pain and heartache. I hope instead of being embarrassed by the events in this book that instead you, too, can use it to gather your own strength knowing that you, too, were born into the Unlucky Sperm Club and that you made it to where you are in spite of your membership. I love you all.

To my wife, Skye, you have helped me become a better version of myself than I ever realized was possible. You are truly my soulmate.

To my three boys, Dawson, Branson, and Grayson, I have so much respect and admiration for what type of young men you are. You are all so different but yet the same. You young men have given me the hope that this world can become a better place because of you and others like you. Always remember who you are and the potential that lies within you.

To my mom, Diane Burns. As difficult as my early life was, I know that it does not compare to the life that you lived. You are the true hero in this story.

To my dad, Pat Burns. Thank you from the bottom of my heart for allowing my mom to live her happily ever after.

To my brothers, Jimmy, Curt, and Leroy, and my sister, Gloria. I love you all.

To Jeff and Marla Lewis, first thank you for raising such a wonderful daughter. You both have given me the perfect example of what a husband and wife, mother and father, grandma and grandpa, and friend should look like. Not only did I strike gold when I married your daughter but also when you two became my mom and dad.

To Austin, it feels like we have worked together our entire lives, from the window cleaning episode that didn't quite work out to this new adventure of IGOTSMARTER that we are tackling together. I couldn't have done any of it without you. Thank you brother for everything.

To Cindy Gburek, one of the most incredible people I have ever had the honor to work with. You are a true MVP on so many levels. Thank you for everything.

To Uncle Bub, thank you for being you! You are one of a kind!

To all the staff that I have worked with at Doggie District, Bright Child learning centers, FlipNOut Xtreme. Thank you for all your hard work and dedication to help me fulfill my dreams.

To Michael Kammerling, thank you for giving me a chance and my start in the commercial real estate business. This story goes an entirely different direction if not for you and the opportunity you gave me.

To Mike Zobrist and Scott Price, thank you for always making me look good and doing most of the heavy lifting.

To Chuck and Mary Diacont, their families and friends, thank you for giving me role models when I needed them the most.

The Weaver family, thank you for being the family I needed when I needed it.

Thank you to all the others that I don't have room to thank by name. You know who you are. You're the one saying, "Why didn't he mention me?" I know, I should have mentioned you by name, I am sorry. A sure fire way to fix that is for you and all of your friends and family to buy this book and give it great reviews so that I get to write another book, and I promise if you do that I will mention you by name. Seriously, there have been so many people who have touched my life that I could fill pages and pages of the people that I am grateful for. You really do know who you are, and I really am eternally grateful for you in my life.

Table of Contents

Chapter 1

Welcome to the Unlucky Sperm Club

*"We cannot become what we want to be
by remaining what we are."*

— **Max De Pree**

"You better turn on Fox News right now," Aaron said in a panicked voice on the other end of the line.

I flicked on the television. A reporter stared back at me, smiling and clutching her microphone. Beneath her, big white letters read, "Day Care Employee Arrested on Child Molestation Charges."

"Are you seeing this?" Aaron asked.

I had forgotten I was still on the line.

In the upper left-hand of the screen was the name "Bright Child Learning Centers." On any other day, this may have been the kind of news I numbly processed as I questioned what is wrong with the world. But today, this news was significant: *I* owned a chain of six day care centers called Bright Child Learning Centers. I stared at the alleged child molester's photo as he flashed up on the screen. This was the mugshot of the director of one of my centers, a man whom I had hired and trusted. The director's job was above all else to keep the children safe. *Oh, my goodness, what have I done?*

I had always scoffed when I heard people say, "My knees buckled under the stress of the moment," but in that moment, I found out it was a real phenomenon. I dropped to the floor, almost in slow motion.

"I'll talk to you later," I told Aaron, and hung up the phone.

Have you ever told yourself, "At least things can't get any worse"? Yeah, don't do it! I had been fighting the universe over the past few years trying to hang on to everything that was good in my life, and each time I thought to myself things couldn't get any worse, they did! I should not have been that surprised to see my day care center on the screen with a child molester's mugshot plastered next to it. For that matter, I wouldn't have been surprised to see one of my day care centers engulfed in flames after being hit by a meteor.

The global financial crisis of 2008 had destroyed most of my business deals and consequently my life. As a commercial real estate broker and investor, I lost millions in real estate deals and commissions. And I had just ventured into investing in and starting businesses. I had invested in a chain of children's day care centers that I was running and managing. Those very day care centers now had me on my knees in my living room trying to catch my breath. I'll get into how I came to be managing a business I knew nothing about—and frankly didn't *want* to know anything about—later.

I had also started an upscale doggie day care and boarding business. That business was finally starting to do well right as the 2008 meltdown collided with my plans of prosperity. Of course, the upscale dog-boarding business depended on people having disposable income to take vacations with, money to spend up to $100 a night for their dog's stay with. (That stay occurred in a luxury suite, with all day indoor/outdoor play, swimming pools, and, of course, a bedtime story complete with a tuck-in service and nighttime belly rub.)

As bleak as my professional life looked, my personal life was even worse: my marriage was on life support after having been brought back from the dead several times over the last few years.

Silly me—after three years of fighting for everything, I was beginning to think I had made it out of this perfect storm that destroyed lives and fortunes with ease.

Alas, fortune wasn't meant for me. I'm a member of the Unlucky Sperm Club. I'm not supposed to have any kind of success in my life. As with most members of the Unlucky Sperm Club, the foundation for the circumstances of my life were laid before I was even born. If you are a member of this unheralded club, you know exactly what I am talking about.

The Unlucky Sperm Club consists of the people who were born into a situation that has crippled their upward economic and social mobility from the day they were born. The criteria is lengthy and varied, from being born into extreme poverty to having abusive parents. Or maybe you were born with learning or physical disabilities. Maybe to a teenage mother, and then deprived of a relationship with your father. The list could go on and on, but the fact is, members know what criteria put them in "the club."

Me, I could check most of the boxes that guarantee membership in the Unlucky Sperm Club.

I guess I need to give you some background so you have the full picture. We should probably start with the murder.

It all started in a small town in central Pennsylvania just a few miles away from Penn State University in October 1971. The fall foliage was in spectacular bloom as jack-o'-lanterns kept watch on front porches of Bellefonte, Pennsylvania. The beautiful Victorian-style community consisted of about 6,000 salt-of-the-earth, hard-working residents. The town was built in the late 1700s and early 1800s. There was a gorgeous park on one end of Main Street and a magnificent white courthouse on the other end.

That October, one man's actions would mar the peaceful community. That man was Johnny, the local trash collector. Johnny was an imposing, solid tree of a man. And Johnny had a glass eye that seemed to look right through those who dared to look at him.

3

Johnny fit every town bully stereotype you could drum up. He dropped out of school before finishing the fifth grade. He was an alcoholic and a womanizer. His 15 children lived on the outskirts of town in a small three-bedroom house that lacked an indoor bathroom. Johnny would frequently get involved in barroom brawls or assault traveling salesmen who had the misfortune of calling upon his wife, Gloria, to sell their wares. No one wanted to be on his bad side.

For the most part, people steered clear of Johnny. That gave him permission to behave however he wanted, with no real repercussions. That is, until a little thing called conservation started working its way into the headlines. Environmental issues started taking precedence in the media in the early 1970s, and communities started to crack down on people who were not environmentally friendly. What better a place to enforce environmental codes than charming Bellefonte?

Johnny owned a piece of land that was three miles outside of the town. His property served as a landfill where his garbage trucks dumped their daily loads. He had been warned several times to bring his landfill up to code or it would be shut down and he'd have to dump his trash at a new state-run landfill. But Johnny didn't have to follow the rules, so he ignored the warnings and did business as usual.

Fed up with his belligerent ignorance, the local magistrate pushed the issue and smacked Johnny with a citation to cease and desist operations of his landfill. One can only imagine the scene in the sheriff's office when the official injunction notice had to be delivered. Perhaps, the men drew straws to determine who among them would have to confront the notoriously surly Johnny. No one wanted to rile him. No one. The unlucky few had to go to Johnny's land where he dumped the trash. I imagine many threats and obscenities were uttered. They went to poke the bear and that bear got angry.

They say every man has his breaking point. It is a pivotal moment, much like my short-circuit of nerves as I witnessed the public announcement of my child care director's new title of "child molester." Some men break down and cry. Other men puff up their chests and prepare for a fight. I bet you can guess which man Johnny was. But the citation wasn't Johnny's breaking point. No, it was something much worse.

The story I've been told many times goes something like this: A few hours went by after the citation was served. Johnny sat on his porch drinking beer after beer. At some point, he went inside the house and ran into his daughter. Moments later he stormed out of the house with a fistful of ammunition and several guns tucked under his arm. These were three things Johnny had plenty of: beer, guns, and anger.

Johnny stormed down the porch and threw the guns and ammo into the passenger seat of his car. His wife, Gloria, startled by the commotion, begged him to put the guns away and go upstairs to "sleep it off." But she didn't push it too far because it was not uncommon for Johnny to take out his frustrations on herself and the children. She was no stranger to what Johnny could do when he was mad and drunk. She had worn the proof on her face many times.

The engine roared to life, drowning out Gloria's desperate pleas. Johnny's car tires kicked up gravel and dust as he whipped the car around and sped off, swerving ever so slightly. Gloria stood helpless, wringing her hands and silently praying Johnny wouldn't hurt anyone as she watched the car disappear down the road.

Moments later, Johnny's car barreled into the downtown area and made a beeline towards the county courthouse.

Outside the courthouse a young police officer and an auxiliary officer directed traffic. Johnny slowed as he saw the two officers standing only 50 yards away. He pulled to the side of the street and stopped where he had an unobstructed view of the two men directing traffic. Johnny reached into the passenger seat, pulled over his rifle, stuck it out the window and pointed it toward the police officers, opening fire. Pedestrians ran for cover, many hitting the ground. A couple stood frozen in place by fear and shock as Johnny fired off shots left and right.

A young mother ran with her baby carriage around the side of the courthouse seeking refuge from the rain of bullets. Men and women tucked themselves behind cars or ran toward the courthouse doors. Papers flew through the air like confetti as purses, briefcases, even shoes were left behind in the mayhem. Screams and gunfire rang out from all directions. Hazy smoke hung over the bedlam and confusion.

"My Gosh!" a woman shrieked as she ran from a nearby store into the street. "It's Clarence! No!"

Betty Seaward crashed down next to a policeman lying on the ground. A bright crimson pool grew around the body of her husband, 45-year-old auxiliary officer, Clarence Seaward. He was shot in the shoulder and critically wounded, just yards away from another officer, 29-year-old Ronald Seymore.

The shots stopped, and Johnny's car sped off. Sirens wailed and blue-and-white flashes of light descended upon the courthouse. Word spread quickly through town. When Gloria heard there had been a shooting at the courthouse, she knew it was what she had feared the most.

"One young officer is dead," someone told her. "The other one is on his way to the hospital in Hershey."

Officer Ronald Seymore, father of five young children, succumbed to his wounds. Mayor Keller appeared on television to confirm the shooting and assure the townspeople that the sheriff was close to apprehending the shooter. Hours later, at about 10:30 p.m., deputies closed in on a hunting cabin in the woods some 40 miles northeast of Bellefonte. Johnny was waiting for them, but by this time he had sobered up. Dozens of police surrounded the cabin just waiting for the man inside to give them a reason to exact their revenge for their fallen brother-in-arms, but Johnny was taken into custody without incident.

Johnny the trash collector was charged with murder and assault with the intent to kill. He was held at the penitentiary in Rockview while he awaited trial. The *Express* of Lock Haven quoted Johnny saying that he wasn't sorry for what he did, and they could just take him out back and hang him. Many residents of Bellefonte wanted to do just that. But they were scared. No one wanted to take the stand and tell a jury they heard

Johnny's threats or had seen him bully people. Police were left with no other options than to confront Johnny and determine where the tragedy had escalated from.

At first, the local newspapers carried the story. Then it spread to other outlets. Even the *New York Times* picked up the story of the cop killer from Bellefonte. The trial date was set, and the attorneys squared off in the biggest case that had ever taken place in Bellefonte. Everyone thought it would be an open-and-shut case, with or without the witnesses. Johnny would get what he deserved and be sentenced to death for shooting two law enforcement officers.

The prosecutor laid out the evidence and presented the case. A select few individuals were willing to testify against Johnny, recounting the horrific scene. The prosecution rested, confident they had done more than enough to convince the jury to return with a guilty verdict. The defense called several witnesses before their final one, Diane, Johnny's 16-year-old-daughter. Diane had just given birth to a baby boy. Through tears and sobs she recounted to the jury the real reason her father had done the horrible things he had done: She testified that, nearly a year earlier at the age of 15, she had been raped by Officer Ronald Seymore after being pulled over for a traffic stop. She had finally told Johnny what had happened the day of the shootings. Jonny had become so enraged that he went out of his mind.

The defense asked the jury, "Who wouldn't be, after hearing what happened to their 15-year-old daughter?" Johnny had taken justice into his own hands. Diane's tearful testimony continued. She felt like this entire situation was her fault. If she had never told anybody, none of this would have happened. Now Officer Seymore was dead and her father was facing the death penalty for killing him.

Gasps rang out throughout the courtroom. It was a testimony no one expected. Sure, Diane got pregnant at a young age, but no one had known who the father was. With the news brought to light, confusion and doubt filled the room. Residents of Bellefonte were split and so was the jury. Some thought Johnny should pay. Others felt the whole thing was tragic, but Johnny was somehow justified in his actions, for once. The conflict led to a hung jury.

A new trial was set, and the prosecution was prepared to refute the allegations that Officer Seymore had raped Johnny's 15-year-old daughter. Diane's testimony and the hung jury meant the prosecution no longer sought the death penalty. They switched their goal to life in prison without the possibility of parole. Whether or not Officer Seymore had raped Diane was not the issue the prosecution argued. The fact that a young police officer was dead was the issue. There was no justification for taking the law into your own hands, even under the circumstances that the defense alleged had happened.

This time, Johnny was found guilty and sentenced to life in prison without the possibility of parole. Officer Seymore's wife moved away with her family, wanting to get as far away from that town as she could. Johnny's family, including his wife and 15 children, didn't have the money or energy to move after the trial. Some of Johnny's children were adults with families of their own. So they stayed put to deal with the aftermath. Diane and her new baby would forever be labeled and judged in Bellefonte.

So how does this unfortunate story relate to my induction into the Unlucky Sperm Club? Well, Johnny was my grandfather. Diane was my mother. The baby used as a pawn in the most infamous trial in Bellefonte history was me. It created a living nightmare for my early life, and thus, I became a fully initiated member of the Unlucky Sperm Club.

Fortunately, membership in the Unlucky Sperm Club, if used properly, could be your greatest resource toward living a successful and productive life. I have proven that by using goals and personal development techniques and strategies that no matter what circumstances you find yourself in, you can create the life that you desire. As you will learn in this book, it's not easy—but it is possible. Not only is it possible, it is *probable*. I truly believe that If you have enough time, focus, and energy you can accomplish anything!

Chapter 2

In This Business, We Kiss Dogs

"Always make your future bigger than your past."

— Dan Sullivan

Just a short few years before I saw the broadcast on the news, I felt like everything in my life was coming together. The roll call of my successes was quite lengthy and only getting longer, especially considering I was a member of the Unlucky Sperm Club. I had spent years working and learning the commercial real estate industry. I'd become a respected industry leader. I had just been named the number one broker worldwide for Grubb & Ellis in their retail division. Not only had I done well on the brokerage side of commercial real estate, I had developed several commercial properties on my own as well.

To slap the cherry on top of the cake, my wife, Skye, and I had three sons, and our family felt perfect. My children, Dawson and Branson, attended good schools and played baseball and soccer. My youngest, Grayson, was already showing off his giant personality as a healthy two-year-old. It was the quintessential American Dream.

I was working on $200 million worth of deals as a commercial real estate broker. I had eight different shopping centers in various stages of construction under contract to be sold. The future looked bright. I wouldn't get paid a penny until the deals closed, though, and in fact, some of these deals had me investing my own money alongside the actual investors and developers.

I spent years investing in many commercial real estate projects that spat out passive income every month. I was a yes man: When somebody approached me with an investment, I said yes. Yeah, I'll get in. Yes, I'll do that. In my mind, every investment was going to work out, and I was going to make a lot of money. I had this goal of building up all these different streams of revenue so that multiple streams of investment profits would pour into my bank accounts each month. I could see myself walking to the mailbox each month with a big cheesy smile on my face, collecting all the disbursement checks, and not worrying about money ever again. It would be a life that was a stark contrast from my own upbringing.

But let's get back to my "yes man" mentality. I was so much of a "yes man" that I started to look outside of commercial real estate to invest and began to consider investing in businesses. This "yes man" mentality was what had me on my knees in front of the TV trying to catch my breath. Day cares were a great investment when I started investing in them, so much so that my success there emboldened me to try other business investments.

I purchased a vacant building that had been used as a day care until a new day care operator opened up directly across the street in a state-of-the-art facility. They drove the operator of the original day care out of business, so the building was for sale cheap. While I was trying to find a fast-food tenant to lease the property, I was approached by a tenant who wanted to open up a doggie day care business. I almost laughed. A doggie day care? What the heck is that? She explained to me that it was a new trend that was growing in popularity across the country. I was a yes man but I wasn't stupid. I didn't care how popular these alleged dog day cares were. There was no way I'd lease the space to somebody opening a doggie day care. I didn't think that business would last a month, let alone the five years needed to fulfill a commercial lease.

She asked if I would meet with her and her partner to discuss the possibility of them leasing the space from me. I said yes to the meeting more for entertainment purposes than to seriously consider it. She and her partner explained to me the business model and provided me with a pro forma regarding the industry and the type of money they anticipated making. She did a great job pitching the concept to me; so much so that I did a little of my own research on the doggie day care business, and suddenly, it no longer felt like a joke.

In fact, I had to admit it looked like that type of business was catching on and it could make a viable tenant for the space. I started to seriously negotiate with the tenant to occupy the space with her doggie day care. As the negotiations continued, I started to get excited. I could envision the dogs playing at the building. The day care tenant had left behind all the outdoor play equipment and shade structures that the kids had used. The dogs would love that yard as much as the kids did. It was going to be perfect.

But the negotiations broke down when the doggie day care tenant found a space that she thought would be better for her business. By this time, I had sold myself on the doggie day care business and industry. This shows you my state of mind. I was a dealmaker. I had gone from laughing at the mere fact of having a doggie day care as a tenant to contemplating opening one myself. Forget the fact that I had no operational experience in any business, let alone the doggie day care business.

It was 2005 and I was living in a world where you just had to build it and people came. Or, in this case, I was hoping dogs would come. It worked for Kevin Costner in *Field of Dreams*, right? The economy was on fire. Businesses were making money hand over fist. You couldn't lose. So I said to myself, screw it, I can do this. I had three dogs myself; how hard could it be?

I spent the next few months learning everything I could about the doggie day care and the dog boarding business. I was still working 60-hour weeks as a commercial real estate broker, so after my kids went to sleep, I surfed the web, watching videos and reading any article I could find on my new industry. When I was convinced that I knew everything there was to know about the business, I pulled the trigger on the construction. The building was between where I lived and where my real estate office was located, so I could check in on the construction in the morning before I went to work and again in the evening when I came home.

Once the construction was complete, I hired a manager and staff from Craigslist. I had no idea what to look for or how to hire anyone. I mean, come on, if you could find a good coffee table on Craigslist, why not a decent doggie day care staff member? If the applicant had any experience with animals whatsoever, I hired them. Any animal experience was more than I had, let alone any experience running a business. I hired everyone that showed up for their interview and thought I had hit the jackpot when one of the applicants had six years of experience as a kennel technician. I hired her to manage the entire operation. Almost immediately I realized I had made a huge mistake. Well, multiple mistakes. One was my hiring practices. The second was the business itself. It seemed that the Las Vegas Market was not ready for a doggie day care. No matter how low our prices were, we couldn't get more than 10 to12 dogs a day, and I needed 55 dogs a day to break even.

Ever the dealmaker, I continued to throw money at this business for six months until I realized that it was not going to make it. I decided I had had enough and that I was going to shut down the business and try and find a fast-food tenant after all. Believe it or not, I lost more money in one year on my first business venture on my own than I had made in the first 27 years of life combined. I was sick and discouraged beyond belief. But then I remembered my brother-in-law, Austin Lewis. He was my administrative assistant, my right-hand man at my commercial real estate business.

Austin loved animals and had actually worked at a vet's office through high school in the boarding department. He'd even wanted to be a veterinarian at one point, until he realized he didn't have the heart to see animals sick or injured every day. Ultimately, he decided against pursuing the vet career, but Austin had more animal-handling experience than anyone that I had hired, with the exception of the manager.

Wait. I can't run this thing but Austin could. My "never say die" mentality pushed me to talk to him. I asked Austin if he would be willing to go in and run the business as the manager until we could find a new one. I told him I would pay him the same salary to run the pet resort as I did to work with me in commercial real estate. He was not excited at first. He was young, 26 years old, wet behind the ears, just married, with no managerial experience.

With much persuasion and even a little begging, he was willing to give it a shot for a few weeks until I was able to find a better manager. His only condition was that he didn't have to fire the existing staff that worked there. Austin was always careful to make sure everyone liked him. I agreed that I would do the firing to spare Austin the experience. We got into our cars and drove to the pet resort. Not only did Austin not want to fire anyone, he didn't even want to be in the same building when I did it. He drove around the block and stayed in the car until I called him to tell him that it was done.

Standing in the pet resort, Austin looked so professional in his suit and tie, since he'd originally thought he would be at the commercial real estate office for the day. Instead, he spent the day getting to know the building, the remaining employees, and the few dogs we had in that day. I returned to my real estate office to continue my work. At the end of the day, I came back by the pet resort. Austin looked like he aged five years in five hours. He was literally a fish out of water running a pet resort and had no idea how to do it. His tie was gone. His suit was dirty. But he stuck it out that first day.

The very next day he woke up at 5:00 a.m. and went into the pet resort, this time in jeans, to open up "Doggie District Pet Resort." He tried his best to make it work. Days turned into weeks. Weeks turned into months. And the longer Austin was there, the more comfortable he got with the business. He started to like it. And eventually something strange happened. The business started to take off. Austin became a master at customer service and people just loved him. They knew how much he loved their dogs. Austin made everyone feel special. He knew all the customers' names, where they worked, where they vacationed, what their favorite color was, how their spouse had irritated them that morning, and a thousand other pieces of personal information. In fact, some customers shared way too much information with him, and Austin realized that it takes all kinds of people to make this world interesting.

As much as he made the customers feel special, that was nothing compared to how he treated their dogs. Not only did he know all the dogs' names, he gave most of the dogs nicknames. Austin treated these dogs like they were his family. When they came through the door, the dogs would sprint to see their Uncle Austin. He would get down on the floor and give each dog a kiss and a belly rub. He was really in his element. I had to laugh. A few months earlier, Austin was working in a professional office, dressed in a suit and tie. He was concerned about whether his shoes had a good shine or not. Now he was in jeans covered in dog hair and drool, kneeling on the floor, French-kissing English bull-dogs and German Shepherds.

Eventually, customers started to feel guilty if they didn't take their dogs to see Uncle Austin. We went from five or 10 dogs a day to 30 or 40 dogs a day. One night, Austin called me at 9:00 p.m. I was so worried when I saw his number on the caller ID. We had had a few issues with dogs being injured in fights with other dogs so I just assumed another situation had occurred.

"Hey, it's me," he said, cheerful as ever.

I breathed a sigh of relief. "What's up, Uncle Austin?" That was our new joke.

"Do you want to know how much we made today?" he asked.

"Sure, was it a good day?"

"It was. We went over $1,000. We did it!" he exclaimed. The fact that we could earn $1,000 in a day was mind-blowing to both of us. We were making $75 to $100 a day from the business before Austin took over man-aging it.

He loved it so much he decided he didn't want to come back to the real estate industry. He had found his passion so I made him a partner. I thought we were going to print money with Doggie District, the same way we were printing money with the Sweet Pea day care investments for the last few years.

That Sweet Pea investment was what started this entire chain of events with the businesses and me thinking that anyone could make money running a business.

While doing commercial real estate, I started out leasing spaces out for landlords. They would hire me on the listing side of their properties. I would then market their projects to all the other agents and tenants to fill up their vacancies at the shopping centers. Because the Las Vegas market was so strong and Vegas was growing so fast, there was not much standing inventory when it came to retail real estate. Whatever shopping centers that were built would quickly be leased out by tenants. That had developers buying land and giving the listings to brokers before the buildings were built. This is called a pre-construction listing: a pre-construction listing is exactly what it sounds like—no vertical construction has been done on the site.

Banks required a certain amount of pre-leasing—executed leases with tenants before granting a construction loan to build the shopping center. The banks wanted to make sure there were enough tenants with signed leases to cover the mortgage before they loaned any money to build a shopping center. So developers had to get a few tenants to sign leases before the construction could start. Most banks required 40 percent of the shopping center be pre-leased before the bank would release the funds for vertical construction.

Pre-leasing an unanchored shopping center was the most difficult assignment in commercial real estate. Tenants were very apprehensive to sign a lease before they saw any construction on the site. Many a tenant has waited a year or longer, past the promised delivery date for a project that they signed a lease on before construction started, all along possibly missing out on other opportunities to lease space in the same area. I had a few of these listings. I had to strategize what types of businesses would really work in these pre-construction spaces. Las Vegas was growing quickly and many families in Vegas comprised hardworking parents with children. Day cares in Vegas were busting at the seams. When I noticed this trend, I started cold-calling day cares and pitching retail sites to them. After many attempts, I came across Sweet Pea Learning Centers. They had two other locations at the time and had plans to expand.

I pitched a space to Sweet Pea, and they wanted in. Feverishly, I got the deal done and signed. Six months later, I landed another site that would work perfectly for a day care. I returned to Sweet Pea and told them what kind of deal I could get them. They loved it, but there was a catch. Apparently, it costs $200,000 to $300,000 to start a day care from the ground up. That includes furniture, fixtures, and equipment, basically everything.

"I'm sorry, I just don't have that," the owner told me. "I'm going to have to wait another year to even get to that point."

I found my entrepreneurial senses tingling. This was a great opportunity and I wanted to see it work. I went back to the Sweet Pea owner and said, "It is a great deal, and someone is going to get in there. What if you found some investors who could fund the setup and operational start-up for you? Would you be willing to do the deal then?"

"Yes! Of course!" he said. That meant he could start a business with no money out of his own pocket and grow at a rapid rate.

Success. I had just started to make some decent money by this time. My father-in-law, a local dentist, once told me if I ever came across a good investment to let him know because he had some money to invest. This felt like the perfect investment opportunity. I talked to him about the investment, and together we met with the owner of Sweet Pea. The three of us came up with a deal to where my father-in-law and I would fund 100 percent of the start-up costs and the owner of Sweet Pea would run it.

We came across other deals for Sweet Pea where we could do the exact same thing. Together we got to the point where we had six day cares up and operating through this partnership. My father-in-law and I would front the cash, and the Sweet Pea owner would run the business side. In turn we'd get paid monthly or quarterly disbursements depending on how well the day cares did. And it worked really well. We were getting four to five checks a month with excellent returns on our money. It felt like a no-brainer.

Even though I was patting myself on the back, success was still a foreign experience for me. My American Dream was still overshadowed by my humble and at times downright stressful beginnings. My formative years taught me many lessons and forced me to create the luck I have today. But let me tell you, my childhood wasn't a cakewalk. I credit many of those experiences for my tenacity and resourcefulness today.

When you're the outcast kid in an impoverished family, you generate whispers and stares wherever you go. So I blocked out my humble beginnings for the most part, burying the trauma of them in my heart, even in the wake of my success. These feelings of being "different" stayed dormant until something traumatic, like my day care director crisis, stirred the memories up.

But the memories were always there, just below the surface. Growing up, my grandmother, Gloria (we called her "Gram"), and most of our immediate family lived on a cul-de-sac. It ran straight down the road until you couldn't go any further. At the end of the street there was a huge drainage ditch that ran underneath some train tracks. The street was flanked on both sides with gypsum factories, one a mile to the east and another four miles to the west. These factories spat out billowing plumes of smoke that layered everything within five miles of them with gypsum dust. Glamorous, I know.

Since there wasn't much to do on our street, we made our own fun. It was tradition for the entire family to gather on my grandmother's porch in the afternoon and watch the cars go up and down the street. Now there were only eight houses down the road of that dead-end street so there was not much traffic. It was a great treat to see a new car. Oh, the excitement!

One summer, my cousins Brian, Ralphie, our friend Jon Emel, and I decided to increase our odds of new cars going up and down our dead-end street. About half a mile away, the town was doing some construction on the road. There was a huge detour sign with an arrow pointing the intended direction and flashing lights on the top. On a boring Saturday morning, we noticed the construction crew wasn't working, so we "borrowed" the detour sign and put it directly by Gram's street entrance. Every car that came up and down saw the sign and was forced to turn down our dead-end street.

It was hilarious. We got to watch about eight to 12 cars an hour, a big increase from a typical Saturday morning. We received every reaction imaginable. Some drivers shook their heads laughing, realizing they had been duped by four boys. Others were not as amused. They flipped us off and yelled at us through their car window.

This was fun for about an hour but the luster wore off. As he usually did, Ralphie upped the ante by pulling down his pants to moon the cars that drove by. Soon those passing by were not just seeing one boy mooning but four moons as they traversed the phony detour. As the day went on, we became bolder. Mooning wasn't enough. It got to the point where Brian and Ralphie would pull down their pants and stick their butts high in the air. Me and Jon Emel would play the "Butt Drums," swinging our arms and heads to the music. The looks on those poor people's faces were priceless. Years later, I can still see their shock—and, well, disgust.

Eventually, someone must have called the police, because several cars later an ominous unmarked brown Dodge slowly came down the road. We took off running for the back green, the field behind Gram's house, and hid the rest of the day. We were terrified to go home, fearing the police had knocked on Gram's door and told her what we did. Somehow, we never did get caught.

To this day, it is one of the funniest memories I can recall from my childhood. We saw many people who lived less than a mile away from Gram and knew exactly what street they were turning down. They knew it led nowhere but were willing to follow the sign because it was there. It was almost as if they were going throughout their day unconscious, just doing what they were told to do and following the proverbial signs of life. They were not putting any real thought into what they were doing. To make things worse, after knowing they had done something unwise, on their way back up the dead-end street they had to see and hear the "Butt Drum" band.

As the world was unraveling all around me, I couldn't help but think that if I would have taken just a second to think about what signs I was seeing before I went all-in on the day cares, I wouldn't be looking down a dead-end street now, having to hear the "Butt Drum" band in the background.

Chapter 3

Necessity Breeds Resourcefulness

"It's not the lack of resources that cause failure, it's the lack of resourcefulness that causes failure."

— **Tony Robbins**

I was too happy building my empire and making money for either me or my father-in-law to see the signs. Even though I lived well within my means, I could still support my family's every wish. I was the quintessential provider.

From 2000 to 2008, I had a robust partnership with Sweet Pea Learning Centers. We opened five additional locations and I was personally developing and building a building for our sixth. We began construction on the new Sweet Pea building in August 2007. We purchased the land, had the plans drawn and approved through the city, and hired a contractor to get building. It was exciting, creating something new from the ground up and trying my hand at development. It also foretold of additional income and profitability. The other centers were doing great. If it isn't broke, don't fix it.

It is hard to pinpoint exactly when the word "recession" began to tumble out of people's mouths. It was a scandalous whisper, an unheeded warning, a futuristic implausibility in the new millennium. Or so we thought.

I had no idea just how much my world would be turned upside down. I was simply in the moment, trying to expand on my resources as much as possible. After all, we Tresslers had to be resourceful.

But I wasn't going to panic, at least not yet. When the going gets tough, you need to get resourceful. At least, that is what I remember being told growing up.

I was about eight or nine years old when I heard a knock at the door. I was so excited. Nobody ever knocked on our door. The only people who came to see us were people we knew so well they just walked inside without warning. Eager to see who our visitor was, I ran to the door and threw it wide open. On the other side of the threshold stood a man in a light-brown uniform. A nametag with "Bill" on it was fastened to his shirt above his left breast pocket. I remember it was Bill because I could read the nametag and was really proud of myself for being able to read a word.

I was also relieved that Bill was not a police officer. Bill was not here to arrest anybody. I looked up at him and he smiled down at me, a friendly smile.

"Is Mitzie Tressler home?" he asked me nicely.

I thought about this for a while. Before I could open my mouth again, my mother came up behind me.

"What can I help you with?"

"Hi, is Mitzie Tressler home?" he asked again.

My mom quickly stepped between Bill and I and took over the conversation. I could hear her say something like, "Mitzie wasn't home." But I knew it wasn't true. I had just seen her in the kitchen sitting in her favorite place next to the window with the sun shining on her. I had no idea what Bill wanted with her, so I quickly went to the kitchen to retrieve her and bring her to the door. He looked official enough in his uniform and I figured I better comply with his inquiry.

I returned to the door with Mitzie, our Siamese cat, curled up in my arms and a big smile on my face knowing that my mom and Bill would be proud of me. I made it back to the door just as my mom was trying to end the conversation.

"Is there a time that Mitzie will be home?" Bill asked.

"Probably in a couple of days," my mom replied.

Being the good helper that I was, I quickly wedged myself between my mom and Bill and triumphantly declared, "Mom, here is Mitzie!"

Bill had a strange look on his face while my mother looked down on me in horror. Bill looked at Mitzie and back at my mom and then back at Mitzie again. He shook his head.

"You didn't do that, did you?" Bill said.

My mom turned red. "Yeah, I did."

Bill was from our local power company, and he was there to collect a bill that was three months late. He asked for Mitzie because my mom put the power bill in Mitzie's name. This was before you needed things like a social security number to open a utility account. It wasn't always Mitzie's bill to pay—my mom *had* the bill in her name, but she couldn't pay it, and the power company shut off our power. Once you had an unpaid balance with the power company, they would make you pay it before you could have service turned back on.

My mom didn't have the money the first time to pay the bill. She certainly didn't have three months' worth of money to have it turned back on in her name. So she got resourceful. *Diane* had a balance with the power company but I, her eight-year-old son, didn't have a balance. If she opened a new account in my name, she wouldn't have to pay the balance in *her* name. That got us three more months of power until it was cut off again for nonpayment. Fortunately for us, I had a baby brother. Three more months of power. My mom knew that she had to pay the bill now, at this time she only had me and my brother Jimmy and was pregnant with my brother Curtis. My stepfather, Jim, was in jail at the time, but he probably had a balance with the power company too.

23

She did her best to keep the bill paid, but it was cold that winter. The oil company had a cash-upon-delivery procedure. With no oil, and thus no heat, you could see your breath as you walked around the house during the day because it was so cold. At night it was freezing. My mom put me and Jimmy in bed with her and we covered up with every blanket we had in the house. It was still freezing cold and Jimmy wouldn't stop crying.

My mom grabbed the mattress with all the blankets and dragged it to the kitchen, placing it in front of the stove. She turned on all the burners on the stove to high, turned on the oven, and opened the door halfway. I could feel the heat coming off the stove, but you had to be right on top of it for it to warm you. My mom then took one of the blankets, walked over to the entryway of the kitchen, and nailed the blanket over it so that the entryway was blocked. This prevented most of the heat from escaping the room. Within an hour the kitchen was warm, and my brother Jimmy had fallen fast asleep. It was a fun night for an eight-year-old. I got to sleep in the kitchen and my mom told me it was like a campout and the stove was our fire.

We stayed in the kitchen for a few days. Pennsylvania was going through a cold spell and the outside temperature never went over single digits, dropping well below zero at night. We stayed warm, but I guess a kitchen stove is not the most cost-effective way to heat your house during a cold spell. When my mom got the power bill the following month, she knew she was not going to be able to pay it. Then one day, we had no power and no lights in the house. At this time of my life, turning on the light switches at our house was a real crapshoot. You never knew if they were going to work or not.

A week later, the lights came back on, courtesy of Mitzie Tressler.

My mom definitely taught me how to be resourceful. That was the only way she could get anything done. She never let not having the right, or enough, resources get in her way of getting something done.

A few times a year, Bellefonte had what they called "extra hauling day." This was a special time of year when you could put large items out with your trash and the trash men would take those large items away on select days. If you put big things out and it wasn't an "extra hauling day," the trash men would just leave the items there.

Extra hauling day was our family's favorite holiday of the year.

The extravaganza started the night before, much like how Christmas Eve starts Christmas. The reason for this timing is because people set their trash out the night before the trash men would arrive. In order to get the good stuff, my mom and Jim, my stepfather, would go out around the block checking the curb to see if anything was good. If it was, we'd quickly throw it in the back of the truck and bring home the treasures.

The idea was not exclusive to my family. There were other poor families who lived for extra hauling day. In fact, there were probably about four to six other families, depending on the year, that took this unofficial holiday as seriously as my mom and Jim did. There were six prime streets on "extra hauling day," where all the wealthy people lived. This is where you wanted to be, because you know, wealthy people threw away good things. You didn't want to waste your time on the poor streets because they didn't have anything to throw away. If they did, it wasn't going to be something useful.

If you ever watched the show *Supermarket Sweep,* you know exactly what this night was like. For those who are not familiar with this beloved TV game show, contestants are given a shopping cart. They race through the store to get as many items as they can into their cart, and then they have to return to the register before time expires. Whoever had the most expensive haul won. Contestants ran as fast as they could, often slipping and falling and fighting off asthma attacks. Now if you take that picture and replace the supermarket with a residential street and the shopping carts with pickup trucks, you can vividly imagine extra hauling day.

You had six other families competing to get to the good stuff before the other families got there. Many times, we got to the street of our choosing before dark and sat at the end of the street waiting for the sun to set. This also prevented any of the other families from coming on "our" street. I remember sitting at the end of one of the streets one year, waiting for the sun to set. Another family came driving by with a truck and homemade trailer made out of the bed of another truck. There were five of them in the truck and three on the back of the truck ready to throw as much loot in as they could get their hands on that night. Jim stared them down as they passed. The family knew they would not be able to come down that street and moved right along.

Once it got dark, we'd start our crawl down the street. Someone would drive the truck and the rest of us looked on both sides of the street, running from one trashcan to the next. When you don't have anything, just about *everything* is worth grabbing. We'd grab lots of things that were just "trash." Broken toys that had missing wheels or pieces, worn-out clothes or shoes—but it was better than what we had at home so we took it.

Jim was always scouting the big-ticket items—couches, TVs, bicycles, washing machines, and power tools, just to name a few. Our entire house was furnished from what we would find on extra hauling night. I remember how happy he would be when he found something that was particularly good. Maybe a piece of furniture that was in fair condition or some power tool he thought he could fix. He would put a huge smile on his face and laugh, saying, "One man's trash is another man's treasure," and then eagerly run to the next house in hopes of another big find.

My mother's resourcefulness rubbed off on me. Like I said, it was about survival. When I was about 11 years old, I had three siblings under the age of three. Jimmy was two, Curtis had just turned one, and Leroy was a newborn.

The morning cries, our human alarm clock, usually meant one of my brothers was hungry, had a dirty diaper, or just wanted to get out of his crib. One morning at 6:00 a.m., Leroy was crying hysterically in his crib. I woke up to check on him. His diaper was full so I changed it. He kept crying, though, so I knew he was hungry.

With my brother tucked safely in my arms, I went downstairs and looked around the kitchen to see what I could make a bottle out of. On a great day, we had formula I could heat up on the stove. On a good day, we had sugar, and I'd make sugar water for him. But that day was a bad day. All I could do was give him a pacifier because we had nothing else in the house to give him. I scoured the house, looking for a binky. I went up to his crib and found one between the cushion and the back of his crib. Mind you, he's still screaming all this time.

Once I stuck the binky in his little pink lips, he stopped crying for a while. But when he realized he wasn't getting food, he spat it out and began his earth-shattering screams again. By this time, I was forced to fill a bottle with warm water and give that to him. At least it put something in his stomach.

The pacifier was my go-to tool to get my brothers to stop crying. If they were bored, I'd fetch the pacifier. Hungry? I'd try the pacifier. Bad mood? Pacifier. Once I shoved the binky in their mouth, they would quiet for a short time and sometimes even go back to sleep.

My resourcefulness may have paid off, but little did I know that it would serve as a metaphor for life. Pacifiers work wonders when it comes to quieting a crying child. Unfortunately, though, many adults are pacified *away* from going after their dreams and goals in life. Think about it: How many of us are pacified by that paycheck that arrives every two weeks? It gives us just enough to pay our bills and maybe a few extra dollars to have fun with? Is that job pacifying us just enough to not go out and pursue what we really want to do with our lives? Is it giving us the sensation that we have everything we need and are comfortable in the circumstances we find ourselves in?

Just like Leroy thought, he had what he needed during those first few moments sucking on the pacifier, do we have a false sense of security? What about the relationships we enter into during our lives? Do the people we surround ourselves with, and possibly even love, pacify us to stay where we are because they have no drive or desire to do more with their lives? These are all questions worth considering as you identify the binkies in your own world.

If we take a step back and look at our lives, circumstances, and relationships, we may realize we are born for greater things. We need to take control over our lives and not allow ourselves to be pacified by things that are "just enough."

I realized this once I set out on my self-development crusade. There was so much more in life that I wanted to accomplish. I did not want to allow "good enough" to be good enough in my life. But was that what got me in the situation I was in now? Was that why I was on the verge of losing everything? Did I push too hard; get overly ambitious, prideful, and even greedy? I had always believed that we need to push ourselves to reach our potential, that we owed it to the world to become the best version of ourselves. Had I pushed past that, had I tried to go faster and further then I was capable of? Look where I came from. Did I really have any expectations of being so much more successful then I could have even imagined as I was growing up? The fact that I was not in jail, that I had a job, a great family—shouldn't that have been enough? Why did I have to push so hard? Did I forget that I am a member of the Unlucky Sperm Club?

No. That fact was very prevalent as I looked at my current situation and the unflattering future that awaited me. It was a future that had me losing all that I had built, personally and professionally.

Chapter 4

Pick Your Pain

*"We must all suffer from one of two pains: the pain of discipline
or the pain of regret."*

— Jim Rohn

I remember watching on TV as employees of global investment giant Bear
Stearns walked out of their New York offices clutching cardboard boxes
in 2008. Disbelief and dejection were plastered across their faces. Stearns
went under but it was not alone. Lehman Brothers and many others went
belly up as well. As I witnessed the dominoes falling during the financial
crisis, I tried to stay positive. I had this mentality of, "Well I can't control
the world's economy, but I can control my deals." As the personal-develop-
ment gurus say, you can't control the winds, but you can control how you
set your sails.

That didn't go so well.

In Las Vegas, the people who were building the shopping centers
experienced an abrupt cut-off to their credit, courtesy of the banks. These
developers relied on that credit to build the shopping centers. Without that
credit, and without any new leasing taking place, the banks started calling
the loans and the projects died. Some properties were complete, just sitting

there with no tenants. Others were half-built, with 2 x 4s poking out of the ground like tombstones.

When developers couldn't finish their projects, the investors who put money down up-front in hopes to buy a fully leased shopping center reached out to me. Basically, the conversations went like this, "Hey, the world is ending. Your developer is not going to follow through with construction or reach the 85 percent pre-leasing requirement per the contract. They're in breach of contract. I want my escrow deposit back and I want to cancel the deal." When the investors canceled the deal, it meant that I would not be paid a commission for all the deals I worked on. For years, in some cases. The impact had a ripple effect on everyone.

The construction loans were collateralized with a personal guarantee. These guarantees typically meant you would vouch all your assets as collateral in the case of a default of the loan. Unfortunately for me, I was getting hit from both ends of this storm. Remember that brilliant idea I had to get on the development side of things? Apparently, I had picked the *perfect* time to do that. And by "perfect," I mean "the worst."

Timing is one of those things that can make all the difference. With the right timing, you can look like the smartest person who ever lived. For example, if you buy or sell real estate or stocks at the precise right time, you look like a genius and everyone wants to be just like you. But if you sell or buy that same real estate or stocks at the wrong time, you look like an idiot and people use you as the butt of their jokes. Yes, I'm speaking from personal experience.

One Saturday night at Gram's house, I had a goal to go to the bathroom. But that goal led to a much harder decision that I will never forget. My gram had a lot of people living with her. My Aunt Sue, Gram's youngest child, had one of the two bedrooms. She and her son, Charles, who was about five years younger than me, lived in that room. Down the hallway that led to the bathroom was Candy's room. Candy was the oldest daughter of my Aunt Darlene and Uncle Nelson. Darlene had Candy when she was 16 years old and somehow Candy ended up staying with my gram.

Darlene and Nelson lived in a trailer behind Gram's house with their two other daughters, Kim and Peggy.

My cousins, Brian and John, were also permanent residents at my gram's at this time. John would sleep on the couch downstairs in the living room and Brian would sleep on the loveseat. You just found an empty spot on the floor, put down a few blankets and a pillow, and went to sleep. Space came at a premium but everybody loved staying at Gram's house.

On this particular Saturday night, things were a bit different. Gram's house only had one bathroom. This bathroom got put in two or three years after my pap went to prison. Prior to that, my gram had no indoor bathroom. Apparently, every Sunday night my gram would fill up a galvanized tub with water that she would warm up on the stove and all the kids would get a bath. I remember the outhouse that was at the back of my gram's property. It was a real fine outhouse. It was a "double holer" and by this, I mean there were two holes next to each other inside the outhouse. There was no petition wall separating you, just two holes in the outhouse in case more than one person had to go at the same time. I'm sure this was the case at least some of the time, with 15 brothers and sisters living in this house at the same time.

But back to Saturday night. My cousin Candy was in the bathroom fixing her hair to go out with her friends. Keep in mind, this was the early 80s, and hair was big. Most of my cousins took it to a new level. If you remember Aqua Net hairspray, you would have sworn my cousins were sponsored by the company due to the massive amounts of hairspray they used on their hair. Candy would take hours doing her hair. And for some reason she had to do it without a shirt on, which meant no boys could go in the bathroom.

This would not have been an issue in most situations. Growing up at my gram's, I was never bashful to go to the bathroom outside. But on Saturday I had a bad stomachache and needed to get to the bathroom in the worst way. I pounded on the door telling Candy to open up. I yelled that it was an emergency. She told me to wait. Unfortunately for me, waiting was not an option.

After about 45 seconds of trying to get into the bathroom, I kicked the door right next to the door handle. It was a cheap door, and everybody knew the trick of how to get in when it was locked. Most of the time, we used this when somebody accidentally locked the door. But this time, on the other side of the door, was my naked cousin. I didn't know she was totally naked. She usually sat in there with her bra and underwear on while puffing her hair so high she'd need to stoop to get through any doorway.

I was also certain that, since she'd already been in there for six hours with her pick and six cans of Aqua Net, she would be nearly done. I was "prairie dogging" and I did not want to crap my pants. I kicked the door right in the perfect spot, and it flew open. Naturally, this was to Candy's utter surprise. She stood there, buck naked, with her hair fluffed 36 inches above her head, screaming for me to get out.

I knew at this point I'd screwed up, and suddenly that urgency to go to the bathroom vanished. I hastily shut the door and turned around to head back down the stairs. Candy was still screaming at the top of her lungs. Gram was right there at the top of the stairs, staring at me.

Gram grabbed me by my hair and walked me down the steps. She told me to get on the couch and stay there. Fortunately, for me, this whole episode squelched the urge to have to go to the bathroom. My gram then went up to talk to Candy to try to calm her down and get the story. I'm not sure what Candy told her but Gram came down in a horrible mood. She told me to go out to the lilac tree and pick my switch. This was the first time, and one of the only times, my gram did this to me.

I had heard stories about Gram and Pap making their kids go out and get a switch off the lilac tree so that they could get what was coming to them. This lilac tree grew right at the back door of my gram's house. In the spring it was beautiful. It would have all kinds of purple flowers on it. But now it had become my turn to go pick the infamous switch to get my punishment.

When I first heard Gram say this, I just sat there. I couldn't believe that my sweet grandma was going to give me a switching. My grandma had disciplined me in the past, but most of the time it was her grabbing me by my hair and dragging me to wherever she wanted me to be. Then she'd tell me to stay put. But not this time. When I sat there a second too long, she came over, grabbed me by the hair, and told me to go out and get a switch. She was mad. It was one of the rare times that I had seen her that upset, at least at me. I knew I better go do it.

I walked out the door and stared at the tree. I was horrified. I didn't know which switch to pick. I examined a skinny branch and thought that this might be the one to take to her. It was flimsy, but I thought better of it, imagining that it would feel like getting hit with a horsewhip. I examined the bigger branches but knew that was not what I wanted to be hit with. Then I surveyed something in between. I may have looked at every single branch on that tree because I was out there for about 30 minutes. Tears stung my eyes as I perused the branches.

I was out there so long that Candy's friends pulled up to get her. As she walked out the door, I cursed her. She looked at me just standing there sobbing and agonizing over what switch to pick and then she walked to the car and laughed. "You deserve it," she said.

"Oh yeah, you deserve bigger boobies too," I retorted through my sobs. I ended up picking a switched that looked like it would hurt the least.

As Gram delivered my lashings, it felt like blunt force trauma with a horsewhip at the end. After about three or four, which didn't even come close to the pain I felt agonizing over the choice, I had to sit on the couch for another 15 minutes. Finally, Gram told me to go outside and play. She was never one to hold a grudge.

As I reflect upon this memory, a quote from Jim Rohn comes to mind. Rohn explains that we are going to have one of two pains in our lives. We're either going to have the pain of regret or the pain of discipline. It's up to us to pick. Rohn goes on to say the difference is that discipline weighs ounces while regret weighs tons.

Just as I had a choice of what switch to receive my punishment with, what pain I wanted to fill, all people have a choice of what pain they want to feel because we will eventually feel one of the two pains that Jim Rohn talked about.

The pain of regret is probably one of the most severe pains that any of us will feel in our lives. Many times, there is nothing we can do to change the result we're regretting. It is also a deep pain because we knew that we had other choices. This pain of regret is a tough pill to swallow. And although I'm not sure any of us will ever live a life where we don't have any regrets, we *can* lead a life where we have a lot less regret.

Did we treat our loved ones the way we should've treated them? Did we spend the precious time that we were allotted on the things that really mattered and made a difference? Did we take the risks that were worth taking or did we just stick with the status quo? Are people going to have to lie when they give our eulogy?

If you sat here reading this section and are feeling regrets, it's not too late: We have another choice, and that is the choice of discipline. The choice of discipline is simple. It is doing what you know needs to be done. You have 100 opportunities every day to make the choices that you know you should make, whether it's with your family, your career, or choosing to live the lifestyle that you know you want to live. We are all faced with hundreds of opportunities to make the right choice. We just have to be disciplined enough to make the choices that we know will make a difference.

As news of the financial crisis continued to unfold, I knew I had not been disciplined enough. Even though Sweet Pea day cares were doing fine, it was clear that the growth I was depending on wasn't going to materialize: I hadn't paid enough attention to what was going on all around me. I hadn't planned for the worst, I just hoped for the best. Was this lack of discipline going to leave me full of regret? I was almost certain it was.

The weeks and months following the financial collapse felt like I was staring at that lilac tree all over again, knowing that the pain was coming, and it was up to me to pick what kind it was going to be.

Chapter 5

The F-Word

"Their doubt is your fuel for dreams. You just have to drive."

— **Criss Jami, Healology**

The fallout from the child molester tragedy continued. I was in crisis mode. We wrote letters to all the clients at all six centers explaining the situation and telling them that we'd suspended the director indefinitely. We told our clients that this director had only worked at this one center and didn't have contact with any children from any of our other centers. We also informed all our clients that the police were launching a full investigation into the matter, and asked them to contact the officer in charge immediately if they had any information or felt like their child had been harmed in any way.

The news was leading with this story at the top of every broadcast. The next day, we saw our enrollment drop sharply at every center. I couldn't help but think that I deserved this. I had hired this guy against my intuition. I kept replaying the interviews over and over and my gut feeling not to hire that guy. This horrible choice had sealed my fate and had put the children at our centers in danger. I couldn't take it back no matter how much I wanted to. How many kids had he hurt because of me?

I had reached the point where I wanted to throw my hands up and scream, "It's over, take it all, I'm done." There was nothing I could do to save this business. Everything was lost. I felt like I was in a boxing match with Mike Tyson and he kept taunting me in his high, squeaky voice: "Come On! Come on, fight!" But I wasn't sure I wanted to fight anymore. I had been fighting my entire life to try to escape who I was, where I was born, and what I represented. Over the last three years, I'd fought with all my strength to save everything that I had built and now this.

Life is a lot more challenging when you're not the only one being beat up. I could take the hits. But my wife and kids shouldn't have to bear the brunt of the fight. They lived in a beautiful house with a sport court and swimming pool. Now they'd have to move to a small house or apartment. Even worse than my family having to downsize the house was what would happen to the more than 100 employees of Bright Child. Most of these employees were living paycheck-to-paycheck, and if Bright Child went out of business, they would struggle.

On one hand, I internalized the struggle and felt I deserved it. But on the other, I felt awful for the repercussions my punishment would cause my family and the employees of Bright Child.

The news continued to run with the story. Whenever I'd go anywhere in Las Vegas, people who knew me would do a double take and then look down. They didn't want to acknowledge me. What would they say? Everyone knew about what had happened. It's like having a huge zit on your face that is about to explode or having something in your teeth. People would rather look away than address the uncomfortable situation. They feel bad for you but don't offer words of comfort. I had a few choice words for my situation but I had learned better ones to use.

It was eighth grade geography class. The teacher had a blank map of the United States on the board. None of the names were in the states. Class had just started, and the teacher was pointing to the states, asking if we knew the name that he pointed to. The first state that he pointed to was a square state in the West. Nobody knew what the state was, except me. He was pointing to Utah and the reason that I knew where Utah was on the map was because they had won a national championship in college football a few years before and I had wondered where Utah was. I'd looked it up. I had never been out of the state except once when I was 11 years old: My Big Brother from the Big Brother Big Sister program had taken me to the beach in New Jersey. I wasn't exactly a geographic prodigy.

That was probably the reason I shot my hand up and said "Utah!" before anyone else could say a word. Little did I know that students who guessed the correct state would also have to walk to the front of the class and write the state's name on the map.

I would've never raised my hand if I knew I had to write anything on the board. I'm dyslexic. At that time, I was in the special education classes for reading and spelling. No matter how hard I tried, I could not spell.

When the teacher told me to go to the board and write "Utah," my knees literally became weak and I started to sweat profusely. I stood up and walked to the board. I got to the state of Utah and started by writing a "U," then I wrote a "T," and then I was stumped. I wrote in "H" and then an "L." And then I turned around and sprinted for my seat. Before I made it back, the laughs started. A girl I had a crush on took it to a new level. In a voice loud enough for me to hear, she said, "That's the shortest state name there is, and he couldn't even spell it."

I lost all control. I can't remember exactly what I said, but I let loose a stream of curse words that would've made a room full of sailors blush. I started to call that girl every name in the book. I didn't stop there. I started to tell her how ugly she was, how ugly her mom was, and how stupid her dad was. If the teacher wouldn't have stuck his hand on my shoulder, I would've told her how ugly her grandma was. But the teacher put his hand on my shoulder and politely told me to stop.

My adrenaline was so high at this time, and I was so embarrassed and upset that again I had no control over what was coming out of my mouth. I turned and looked at the teacher and told him, "F&@% you too!" By this time, the tears were starting to seep out of the corners of my eyes. This teacher did not take kindly to the phrase that I had just uttered to him in front of the entire class. His grip became very tight on my shoulder as he squeezed his fingers into my chest and his thumb into my shoulder blade. He picked me up out of my chair.

This was no ordinary teacher. This was Mr. Leathers and he had played major-league baseball for the Phillies. He was a big man. He was the high school varsity baseball coach. And truth be told, he was a really nice guy. But I could almost see the steam coming out of his ears after hearing the phrase I had uttered to him.

He told me to go outside and wait. Everybody knew what this meant. At the time, teachers could actually paddle a kid's butt if we misbehaved. And Mr. Leathers had a reputation that brought fear to everybody at our school. Mr. Leathers had a 30-inch-long paddle that hung next to his desk. One end of the paddle was shaped like the handle of a baseball bat and the other end of the paddle looked as if somebody had flattened out the barrel of the baseball bat. The paddle just hung there next to his desk daring somebody to get out a line. Mr. Leathers prided himself on turning so-called "tough kids" into whimpering children. What Mr. Leathers had done to some of the toughest kids in our school was legendary.

He had made one of them cry big sobbing tears. They said the poor guy was barely able to catch his breath in between sobs. He had hit another one of the tough kids so hard that the kid fell on his knees and started rubbing his butt to try to put out the fire that he was certain was burning in his pants, all while he screamed with pain. If Mr. Leathers considered you a tough guy, he would bring you back into class after the paddling and let everybody see exactly how tough you were. I don't know if he had flashbacks of being at a major-league plate. Perhaps, he had dreams of hitting the game-winning home run when he took that paddle in his hands. I couldn't even imagine how hard he was going to swing that bat at me—I mean, the paddle—considering that I had just told him to F off.

It took him about five minutes to come out into the hall where I was standing. I didn't know if this was a good thing or a bad thing. On the one hand it gave him time to calm down, but on the other hand I had five minutes to imagine every possible scenario of what was going to happen to me when he hit me with that paddle. I envisioned the whole gamut, from him hitting me so hard that it knocked me through the wall and killed me, or him making me cry like a baby and then sitting me in front of the class so the entire school would know that I had cried like a baby. Or—hope above all hope!—him giving me a free pass because of my emotions and what the girl had done to me.

I can still feel my heart dropping as I heard the door open and saw the paddle poking out from the doorway. What I should've done was apologize to him, but my 14-year-old bravado didn't even let me consider that at the time. He always left the door open so the kids in the class could hear the carnage and cries. But they would also hear me begging for mercy if I did ask for forgiveness. There was no way I was going to do that. No matter how bad this paddle hurt, and I was quite certain it was going to hurt, it couldn't be as bad as all my friends ripping on me for the next few months for begging Mr. Leathers not to hit me. *P-p-p-please M-m-m-mister Leathers, don't hit me, I am a wimp.* No, thank you. I would take the whacks.

I just stood there and looked him in the eyes. I could see a little smirk on his face, indicating he was going to enjoy this. He ever so politely asked me to assume the position, which was bent over, hands against the wall, with your butt sticking out like a batting tee. I ended up getting three whacks that day. Fortunately for me, no tears fell, even though it felt like my butt was engulfed in flames. But at the end of the day, this beating wasn't as bad as the beatings that I had endured just a few years earlier from my stepfather, Jim.

The great news for me was that because there were no tears, I was not forced to sit and sob in front of the class. I had taken it as a man. A man with a very hot butt, but a man nonetheless.

My punishment was that I got three days in the time-out program, or TOP. This was in-school detention, where you were separated from all classes and made to sit in a room with all the other juvenile delinquents, knowing that you messed up. Truthfully, it wasn't that bad of a gig. I remember being able to get caught up on a lot of schoolwork that I hadn't done, so it ended up helping me. So I told myself.

After that day, I can remember wanting to not ever swear again, even though it was a way of life in our family. You said the F-word so many times a day it could mean anything, and it was automatic. You said the F-word more than you said "and" and "the." You could use it as a noun, a verb, and an adjective, and in just about any situation. Many times, it was used five or six times in the same sentence. It was quite magical how my family had come up with ways to use the F-word in a wide variety of meanings. And even more surprising was that everybody in town understood exactly what people were talking about. I'm sure to the innocent bystander, it sounded like we were talking in tongues, but to the people in Coleville it was an everyday way of talking.

I tried to curb the F-word, and that lasted for a day before I settled right back into the family ways. Months later, I set out on my second attempt as a child to try to not say the F-word for a complete day. Of course, I was hearing it everywhere. I heard it hanging with my buddies who were saying it (and giving me reasons to say it as well). I think I made it less than an hour that morning before I said it the first time that day. But it wasn't my fault. John Emel had just "cupped a fart" and came up behind me and covered my mouth with it. That not only deserved the F-word but demanded that I use the F-word to tell him how awful that experience had just been. Just as when I had tried earlier, trying not to use that magical four-letter word did not go well for me.

As I write this book over 30 years later, I have finally kicked the habit of swearing. I have found some better words to replace those curse words I depended so heavily on in my youth. That being said, whenever things don't go my way, I do love to use the F-word. It's not the same four-letter word that I blurted out to my teacher when I was 14. This F-word is something much more productive. This F-word is *fuel*.

Fuel is what you use to get the energy and determination to do the necessary things to be successful. If you don't have fuel behind your goals and dreams, it is much like not having fuel in your car.

Others call fuel your "why," but I think they're different, and I think you need both: Having a strong "why" and knowing exactly what it is is one of the most important factors of goal achievement. Paired with fuel, it's a surefire method of achieving your goals.

I have used the F-word "fuel" to help me achieve my life's biggest goals. I never set out on achieving a goal that I didn't have a strong "why" or full tank of fuel. Even if you have a worthwhile goal, it will be hard to accomplish without a full tank. I don't even attempt a goal that I don't have a full tank of fuel for. If I can't come up with a strong-enough "why," chances are that goal was never that important to me and I should focus my efforts on something else.

My wife and children are my biggest suppliers of fuel when it comes to most of my goals. However, I do have some goals that focus around my childhood and the situation I came from. I also draw fuel from all the doubters in my life growing up—all the people who knew with surety that I was never going to amount to anything and all the people who treated me as if I was less than them. I find fuel there so that I can prove to them that I am a good person, that I am worthwhile, and that I am worth their respect. I try to be as creative with the F-word fuel as we were with the F-word in Coleville.

I challenge you to find your fuel in every situation, and use it to propel you throughout your life.

Chapter 6

Know When to Fold 'Em

"You've got to know when to hold 'em. Know when to fold 'em.
Know when to walk away, and know when to run."

— **Kenny Rogers**

Growing up, I was surrounded by Mom's brothers and sisters who had also lived through the hell of their father shooting and killing a police officer in a small town. They, too, were forced to live in the wake of those consequences. One phrase that I heard often from my mom's siblings was, "That's just the way it's meant to be." The declarative phrase was uttered every time something happened and they felt like they had no control over it. The statement was used for a wide variety of things, whether it was after losing a job or if a spouse left. It was as if they felt that life was a game of cards and they had no control over what hand they'd been dealt. They just took the cards as they came and tried to come up with the best hand they could make.

I thought, "That's just the way it's meant to be" was the way life worked. It felt like we had no control over it. However, as I grew older and started to experience life and see that other people were being dealt much better hands, my attitude changed. I saw that we didn't necessarily have to play the hand we'd originally been dealt. Just like in a poker game, we can discard the cards that we don't want.

My mom's family never grasped this concept. They were dealt rough hands, and in many instances, they held on to the hands they'd been dealt. They did the best they could with those cards. I also realized that there were winning hands out there and that all I had to do to was ask for new cards. I don't mean to make it sound like all one has to do is ask and that things will be given. *Asking for new cards* just means making different choices. Those choices may provide a better hand or even a winning hand. In one way, in life it's easier to get a winning hand than in poker: In poker you only get one chance to discard the hand you were dealt. Not so in life.

In life, we get an *infinite number* of times to discard unusable cards and then draw new ones. We do this by constantly making choices. Sometimes if we feel like we have the winning hand, we don't want to discard, we want to just lay our cards on the table and collect our winnings. But sooner or later, life deals us another hand, whether we want it or not. The new hand may come in the form of an unexpected health issue, the loss of a loved one, the failure of the business, or the loss of a job.

Members of the Unlucky Sperm Club sometimes think that a lot of people born into privilege have been dealt a great hand of cards. That winning hand of cards affords them everything that they want in life, so they want for nothing; but unfortunately, the world tends to come in and take that hand of cards and re-deal new ones.

We've all seen it happen with celebrities and the world's elite, who've been born into privilege. The new hand may come in the form of drug addiction, depression, alcoholism, relationship loss, or the end of a star-studded career. People born with a hand they know is not the hand they want to keep are forced to continue to discard the cards that they don't want and draw new ones. That could mean getting an education, starting that business that we've been too afraid to start, or even swallowing our pride and forgiving someone who's wronged us or asking forgiveness from someone whom we've wronged. Each time that we make a new choice, we are dealt a new hand and another opportunity to play and win. The better our choices, the better our cards will be.

Lots of times, while I was growing up, I felt like I'd been dealt many lowly twos and threes, while everyone else had been dealt the aces and the kings. I'm sure many people feel the same way. However, lots of twos and threes can add up to a full house, or to make four-of-a-kind, if we just keep discarding and getting new cards.

So I dedicated my life to making better choices in the hopes of a stronger hand.

Fortunately, I made a few good choices. One of those choices was that I never lived a huge and lavish lifestyle. My real estate buddies bought expensive fun cars and second homes. Once the financial crisis hit, they started to lose those luxuries. Thanks to my humble, dead-end street, dirt-poor beginnings, I lived well within my means. Maybe I lived life subconsciously waiting for the other shoe to drop. Maybe I just didn't feel I needed the bells and whistles that come with wealth and success. I valued simplicity and security and that was all I needed. I also knew from being in the Unlucky Sperm Club how hard life could be.

My fondest childhood memories are rooted in simplicity, like Christmas morning when I was seven years old. I was excited because we had a small Christmas tree, which wasn't always the case. I ran down the stairs, eager to look under the tree and see if there was anything there. I scanned the room and my eyes stopped on my stocking. It wasn't a big red stocking, like the ones you see in movies. No, this was an old, thick, gray hunting sock with a red stripe around the top.

I walked over to it and peered inside. I found an orange, some hard candy, and a few small Matchbox cars. It was perfect! To this day, I can remember the sweet taste of that orange. I peeled it carefully, eating each juicy section as I sat cross-legged beneath the Christmas tree.

I wanted to save the candy so that I could make it last all year. The little Matchbox cars were immediately put to use. I played with them every day until the wheels fell off. I'm not sure there's a Matchbox car in existence that had as much mileage as my cherished few.

What I've realized since that Christmas 40 years ago is that gratitude is not something we gain because of the size or price of the gift that we receive. Gratitude is something we experience because of the attitude we carry within our hearts. Gratitude is the one emotion that can change our life more quickly than any other emotion. As I have pushed myself to be more, and to have more, and to do more, I have also tried to be thankful for all the things that I have been blessed with in my life, both good and not-so-good. If we have an attitude of gratitude, we will be happy in any situation. No matter what our circumstances, and no matter our trials or tribulations, if we keep a sense of gratitude toward all things, we will be happy.

As I sit back to write this book and reflect upon some of the trials that I went through as a boy, I can now find gratitude for the circumstances that I was born into and raised in. Those circumstances have given me the drive and the desire to succeed. They have given me the resolve to work at having a family that doesn't have to deal with the issues that I had to deal with as a boy. They have given me perspective on how things can be if we don't make the proper choices in life. Yes, it is true that I didn't realize that I was grateful for those trials until I was through them. In fact, I'm sure that this is the way it is for most of us. But now, when I'm going through a trial, I stop to think about what I am grateful for *during* the trial. I ask myself, "How is this trial going to teach me or strengthen me, after I get through it?" (I'm looking at you, financial crisis.)

For the last few years, I have kept a gratitude journal. Whenever I feel like life is beating me up, I sit down, and I write down all the things that I am grateful for in life. The more depressed I feel, the deeper I search to find things to be thankful for. I've written down that I'm grateful for things like air to breathe, clean water to drink, food to eat, shoes to wear, and clothes that fit. Some of these things might sound absurd or perhaps too simple, but there are people in the world who don't have clean water to drink, or food to eat, or shoes on their feet, or clothes that fit.

Many of the problems I now deal with are big ones. But dealing with issues like profits being down 5 percent year over year pales in comparison to dealing with problems concerning our health, or divorce, or the death of a loved one. When we are able to put our problems into perspective, it helps us to deal with them more easily. I'm not suggesting that we shouldn't be concerned about profits being down 5 percent. We absolutely should, but we should also realize that it is not the end of the world.

I once did an experiment while our family was headed home from a trip. My boys were in the back seat watching a movie with their headphones on, and my wife had decided to take a nap. We were still three hours from home. As I was driving, as I often do, I started to feel such a great sense of how blessed I was. I had my family and we just had a great trip, staying at a great hotel. We were driving in a good car. I started to give thanks for everything that I could think of in my life. I wanted to see how long I could go on before I ran out of things. It was amazing to realize all the things that came to my mind as I focused on the infinite blessings in my life.

I was thankful for living in a country where I was free and that led me to being thankful for the people who are in the Armed Forces who are willing to put their lives on the line so that I have those freedoms. As the drive continued, I saw two police officers who were dealing with a car that had run off the road. The scene reminded me that I was grateful for the first responders who are willing to risk their own lives for my family. There were construction workers working on the road in 114-degree heat, and I was grateful for them. I was grateful for a car that had air conditioning and tires that were inflated. I was thankful for three boys who could figure out how to argue over *anything* when they were seat-belted into the back seat of a car. The list went on and on and on until my wife woke up about an hour and a half later. I never ran out of things to be grateful for. We can all do ourselves a favor, if we just take the time to count our bountiful blessings.

That includes the cards we've been dealt, too, good or bad. I had been dealt a lousy hand before and made it. But was the problem with Bright Child going to be a situation where the cards I needed were not going to come? Were the cards I needed even still in the deck?

Chapter 7

American Dreams

*"I believe in America because we have great dreams, and because
we have the opportunity to make those dreams come true."*

— Wendell L. Willkie

In 2008, I started construction on a building that Sweet Pea would lease
from me. I wanted my cake and I wanted to eat it too: I would make
money as the landlord *and* as a partner in the business. The construction
on the new building took five months longer than it should have. My original bid was around $2.6 million and then we surpassed $3.1 million. This
development *had* to work out. It had to. I kept hoping the economy would
turn around. I had done deals through 9/11. The economy took a dip a
few months later and then a few months after that it was like the dip never
happened. I remember the dot-com boom and bust. Each time a financial
crisis reared its ugly head, I thought, *In four or five months we'll be through
this. Maybe a year—worst-case scenario.*

People said the financial crisis of 2008 could last five to seven years.
I rolled my eyes and shook my head. They were crazy. This wasn't 1929.
Global markets wouldn't collapse beyond repair. It was bad but it couldn't
be that bad.

We know now that it was even worse than any of us could have imagined.

I was beyond the point of no return. I could not stop construction. Too much money was invested. The loan, the personal guarantee, the eager tenant. The ink was dried, and I just had to see things through. If this project failed, I would lose everything. The bank would take it all. Just as I was finishing the construction, I went to the bank to convert my construction loan into a permanent loan. Construction loans are loans that banks offer on a short-term basis to allow developers to complete construction. If everything goes well, the bank will usually convert that construction loan into a long-term permanent loan with lower interest rates. But right as I was finishing construction and needed to convert the loan to a long-term permanent loan, the economy was crashing and the banks were getting out of any loan that they could. When I called the bank to request permanent financing, the banker didn't exactly laugh at me, but he didn't give me the loan either.

The banker on the other end of the phone said, "Nelson, we are not going to extend or renew your loan or fund any more money toward your project. It is too high risk with everything else that is going on in the market, and frankly, everything that is going on with you." It was shocking to realize that he viewed my life as unpredictable as it felt to me. I tried to keep all the fear I felt buried deep inside of me in hopes that if it was buried deep enough that it would go away. Apparently, I didn't bury it deep enough because the banker was aware that if the economy continued in the direction it was headed, I would be in big trouble. I was now officially labeled high risk even after a decade of doing business together. The journey to securing a loan to complete construction on the Sweet Pea centers was as chaotic and futile it seemed. During a time like this, in the midst of financial mayhem, you really come to realize why bankers get such bad reputations. I continued to plead my case. I told him, "I've been a client of yours for 10 years. I am current on my loan. I did everything I was supposed to do and now you're still going to pull the loan?"

"It's too risky for us," was the line he kept repeating. It didn't matter what I said as I pleaded my case.

"I have just 45 days to secure a loan before you start the foreclosure proceedings. Even though I have made every payment on time?"

"Nelson," he said "Do you have any idea how many banks are going out of business in Las Vegas? Every month a new bank is going out of business, claiming bankruptcy because they have so many real estate loans just like yours, and when people are not able to pay the loans the banks are the ones left holding the bag. Banks need to get out of any real estate loans that we can so we can lessen our exposure to what is coming and try to not be one of those banks that goes out of business. It is a mess. Nelson, it's not personal, it's just business."

"It's going to be personal," I retorted, "when I lose everything after doing everything that I said I would do because you guys have a one-sentence clause in your 35-page loan document saying you can screw me and my family!"

"Nelson, I am sorry. I have to go. It is the Fourth of July weekend and my family and I are going to visit family in Utah."

I sighed. "Well, have a great weekend. I'll start packing up my house while you enjoy your Fourth of July," I said and slammed down the phone.

What was I going to do? How was I going to get the loan I needed to finish the building? I knew I lived in a country where the impossible became possible. I had climbed out of the depths of poverty—why should this be any different? There was always a chance to improve.

Talking to the bank just before the Fourth of July made me think of our own celebrations. One of the greatest days of summer for me had always been Independence Day. Every year, my mom's entire family, which included most of her 14 brothers and sisters, their significant others, and all of their kids would gather at our hunting camp for a party. Every family that ever attended a party at the Tresslers knew that it was expected you arrive with a homemade covered dish of some fashion. It could be macaroni salad, potato salad, three-bean salad (not to be outdone by the five-bean salad one of my aunts would make). There would be pickled eggs, huge pots of mashed potatoes and gravy, baked beans and, of course, lots of desserts of every kind including cheesecake, upside-down pineapple cake, chocolate cake, carrot cake, and anything else you could put a pound of sugar in.

For many years, my Uncle Bub, who took over the garbage route after my pap was sent to prison, would buy a few hundred ears of sweet corn from the Amish and set up his "witch's cauldron," a huge cast-iron pot that could fit 100 ears of corn. He would boil them, and we'd cover them in butter and salt. I'm telling you, there are few things that taste as delicious as sweet corn in July. If times were *really* good, Uncle Bub would buy a pig from the local pig farmer and roast it all night before the big day. Regardless of what food was at the party, there were always a couple kegs of beer.

Every Fourth of July included two main staples of festivities: Playing cards and throwing horseshoes. Most of the time the real festivities involved watching what happened between family members as they played cards and threw horseshoes. Almost without exception, somebody would catch somebody else cheating at cards. Unfortunately, it was usually my mom who got caught. Typically, there would be a huge argument. At best, one or two of the players would stand up, scrape up the dimes and quarters into a pile, and go home with it. At worst, someone would flip the table and a fight would break out. I still have aunts who don't talk to one another 25 years later because of "alleged" cheating at the poker table. That's just one example of how fierce these games were.

As intense as the poker playing could get, the real show was at the horseshoe pit. Only men played horseshoes in my family, and there were huge bragging rights along with the money that was wagered on each game. They would always play partners—four men would play each game two against two. Bets were anything from two dollars a game to five dollars a game. If you skunked the other team, which meant one team got 11 points before the other team even scored, the wager was doubled.

The horseshoe games would go on for hours and hours. Winners would get to stay and play. Losers, after being verbally abused about how bad they sucked, were forced to get back in line if they wanted to play again. The games were very competitive for the first hour or two, but like I said, every party included a few kegs of beer. Red Solo cups sat perched in every man's hand within 50 feet of the horseshoe pit. As the day went on, the beer flowed and the quality of horseshoe throwing deteriorated. But the entertainment quality only got better.

The drunker the man, the more colorful the harassing and badgering.

One thing was certain. There would always be fights when the beer keg was empty. The empty beer keg and fights ranked right up there with Newton's law of gravity: As sure as an apple would fall from the tree, it was just as certain that within 10 or 15 minutes of an empty keg, a fight would break out. My Aunt Sue knew this. On the Fourth of July, you would see her going down to the keg sitting in a cast steel tub surrounded by ice. The more beer the family drank, the lighter the keg. Aunt Sue liked to walk down to the keg and grab it by the tap attached to the top where the beer came out. She'd attempt to lift it. Full, kegs weigh about 150 pounds. Empty, they weigh about 20 pounds. Aunt Sue determined that if she could lift the keg easily with one arm, there were only about 10 or 15 minutes of beer left. At this point, she would pack up her things, get in her car, and drive home. She knew what was coming and wanted no part of it.

I remember sitting near the card table when a fight broke out down at the horseshoe pit. Almost in unison my aunts and the card players would say, "The keg must be kicked." The card playing would stop as they watched grown men punch each other, rolling around on the ground. These fights did not last long. Many of the men were not in the best of shape. In fact, most had beer bellies rolling well over their belts. After about one or two minutes, both men were so fatigued that the fights ended on their own with some cursing and heavy panting. The nature of the damage done to someone determined whether an emergency room trip for stitches was in order or if the men would continue staring and yelling.

Although the fighting and the arguing were highlights of the Fourth of July picnic, the beer keg definitely got the attention of the kids. Especially me and my cousins Brian, Ralphie, and the two Joeys.

The four of us would take turns running up to the keg, ensuring that no one saw us. When the coast was clear, we would fill up a red Solo cup. We would then sprint back into the woods, where no one could see us, and pass the cup around, giving everybody their opportunity to take a long drink. This would continue throughout the day with us alternating who took the risk of filling up the cup. And believe me, it was a risk. If you got caught by one of the uncles, you were definitely getting your butt kicked. Literally. They would pick you up by the arm and kick the back of your butt with the side of their foot and then go on like nothing happened.

One year, I remember my Uncle Allen came prepared with a cooler full of bottled beer. The grown-ups had kept a pretty good eye on the keg that year, and we kids were hard-pressed to get a few glasses. When the keg was kicked, we kids had not had nearly our fill of beer. We took a quick vote and I was voted to try and sneak a bottle of beer out of Uncle Allen's cooler. James Bond would've been proud of my stealth and craftiness. I remember tiptoeing behind the horseshoe pit where everybody was still watching the game. Allen's cooler was four feet behind him, and his eyes were on the game at hand. I nonchalantly walked up and stopped right next to the cooler. When I was positive all eyes were focused on the game, I slowly lifted the cooler lid. I hadn't done enough research on this kind of heist to realize that Allen had the loudest cooler lid in the world. As I lifted it, the creak of the hinges sounded like it could be heard by everybody in the surrounding county even though the sound was barely audible above the noise of the party.

It was as if Allen had trained his ears to pick up that creak no matter how much background noise there was. With the lid halfway open and the creak over and done, I was beyond the point of return. I slid my hand into the cooler just as Uncle Allen turned his head. Our eyes locked. Fear shot through me as if I just stuck a fork in a light socket. I was busted but not defeated. I hastily extracted a longneck from the cooler and began to run. I could hear Allen running behind me. He always had a ring of keys affixed to his belt loop and I could hear those keys rattling in pursuit of me. I ran with all my heart. But no matter how hard I ran I could still hear the keys closing in. When I knew that I was going to be caught I did the only thing

I could think of to save my life—I dropped the beer bottle in hopes that Allen would stop, pick it up, and go back to playing horseshoes. "No harm, no foul." I thought. That was not the case. The keys kept coming, and I could feel Allen closing in.

Just as Allen was about to grab me, suddenly my feet shot out from beneath me and my neck exploded with pain. Allen flew into the air above me, screaming. We had run into a steel wire we used as a fence. Neither one of us saw it. I thought I was going to die. I could not breathe. The next thing I knew Allen was standing above me with fire in his eyes and a nasty bloody line across his stomach where the wire had hit him. He swore at me, grabbed me by the wrist, and lifted me as high as he could. He lifted his boot to the back of my butt, kicked me four or five times, and then for good measure, he smacked me in the back of the head.

The acceptable punishment from a family member to someone else's kid was getting your butt kicked once or twice but never four or five times. Everyone knew it was never acceptable to hit anyone else's kid in the head or face. Allen's adrenaline was elevated from the wire-across-the-stomach situation, so he went above and beyond on the butt-kicking that he gave me. The fireworks were just getting started though. My mom, who had been at the poker table, saw this and quickly got up and started screaming at Allen. She was running down through the field yelling to Allen to stop. Allen did stop and started walking back towards the horse-shoe game. My mom met him halfway, screaming in his face. Mom had fought and won against grown men, so everybody was worried. Fortunately, some of my aunts and uncles came and broke up the fight. As mad as my mom was, if the fight started, Allen may not have made it out of there alive.

All in all, this was a typical Fourth of July party for the Tresslers. However, we never lost sight of what we were celebrating on the Fourth of July. The Tresslers were a lot of things but they were also very patriotic. No matter what circumstances we found ourselves in, we understood how blessed we were to live in the United States of America. My Uncle Gibby had served in the Vietnam War and if the beer was flowing, he would start to tell stories. Not about the battles—I think those were too painful—but about the living conditions of the people in Vietnam and the politics surrounding them. I think everybody understood that things weren't perfect in America but they were sure the heck a lot better than anywhere else in the world. Occasionally, somebody would bring an American flag to the Fourth of July party and stick it in the ground where everybody could see it.

This reverence for country was never lost on me. It was further cemented after I joined the United States Air Force when I was 20. I served overseas in Saudi Arabia and Turkey. The poverty I experienced as a child paled in comparison to the homeless children that I saw on the streets of Turkey, begging for food in hopes of surviving another day. These children were orphans and had no home and no parents and no family. They were left on their own to figure out how to survive. I realized that there were people out there who would have traded places with me in a heartbeat. When I first saw these kids on the streets, I was embarrassed at how upset I had been regarding the conditions of my childhood. This was one of those moments when I can look back and see how my attitude towards my childhood and its circumstances changed and where the self-pity started to dissolve very quickly.

I also saw how women were treated in Saudi Arabia. They were not allowed to show any part of their body except for their hands below the wrist and a narrow slit for their eyes so they could see. I remember standing in a convenience store and there were three or four women in black robes with every inch of their body covered except for their hands and their eyes. When I walked down the aisle they were in, they ran from me. I was told that there were harsh penalties for any woman who was in the same area as another man, let alone an American serviceman.

As bad as things were in the US with the recession and the looming aftermath of the child molester situation, I knew we as Americans were so blessed. I'm not sure anyone who lives in the United States of America can ever use the word "unfortunate" when describing anything. We are so blessed to be living in the land of the free. We are blessed to live in a country that rewards people for hard work and dedication. We are blessed to live in a country where you can be anything that you want to be. This concept absolutely resonated with me. Because I lived in the United States of America, I was not limited by my family or circumstance. The only limits that were placed upon me were placed on me because of me.

Our country is not perfect, but in my opinion, there is no better country to live in that affords somebody the opportunity to succeed as much as they are willing to succeed. We live in a country where we are able to kneel during our national anthem and not be killed or imprisoned. We live in a country where people are able to go from the lowest economic classes to the highest economic classes in the same generation, like I did. Because of this country, I was able to serve in its Armed Forces. And because of this country, I was able to write this book to give other people the hope that they can excel as much as their hard work and determination will take them.

God Bless America!

Now if I could just hang on to all this success through unwilling bankers, a recession, and everything else.

Chapter 8

A Lesson on Contrast

"The greater the contrast, the greater the potential."

— C.G. Jung

I had been denied the loan. And, of course, I had signed a personal guarantee so everything I owned was now at risk. The bank graciously gave me 45 days to secure permanent financing in the toughest financing market since the Great Depression before they would start the foreclosure proceedings. This was a first for me. I went from bank to bank to bank to see if any of them would issue me a loan. Most Las Vegas banks were fighting to just stay in business, so I predictably acquired rejection after rejection after rejection. It was a lost cause. I was about to give up and just start packing our things up and hand over our house to the bank when I saw Andre Agassi and Steffi Graf's smiling faces on a billboard announcing that they had just founded and opened a new bank in Las Vegas and they were lending. Andre and Steffi's bank was new, and they weren't bogged down by bad loans.

I could get the loan but with ridiculous terms and conditions. I ended up paying a 9 percent interest rate because of the perceived high risk of the loan and the borrower. Before the financial crisis, I could get loans for as low as 4.5 percent interest rate, and now I was paying double the interest coupled with huge fees and additional money down on the loan. Beggars can't be choosy. Andre and Steffi had me down Love–40, and I had no other options. But I wasn't going to panic until I had a reason to panic.

As I pulled into the garage of the office at my commercial real estate firm (Grubb & Ellis) and headed to my parking stall, I did a double take at the car parked next to me. This was David's stall. I had worked with David for 10 years. When Grubb & Ellis opened an office in Las Vegas in 1999, David was the first broker they recruited. Michael Kammerling and I were numbers two and three. David was one of the top office brokers in the country and the number-one office broker in our office in Las Vegas. Usually, there was a big, black, shiny S500 Mercedes parked in his spot. But there was no S-series Mercedes parked there. The car was black but it was a Nissan Maxima. I thought to myself that the recession was affecting the Mercedes dealership as bad as the rest of us. They couldn't even afford to give Mercedes as loaners after a fender-bender anymore.

I walked in the door and rounded the corner to head for my office. I could tell something was going on. Over the last year or so, the office had become filled with frustration, disappointment, and in some instances, outright anger. But today the office had a different feel, like somebody had died. I could feel it as I walked past the office staff and a few brokers chit-chatting. As I threw my briefcase on the chair and sat at my desk, my new assistant, Scott, who'd replaced Austin after he'd gone to Doggie District, came into my office and asked me if I had heard the news. "What news?" I replied.

"David lost everything, he had to go bankrupt. They took his Mercedes and his home in Queens Ridge," Scott said. Queens Ridge was one of the exclusive neighborhoods in Las Vegas. It was located in Summerlin on a golf course and was a guarded, gated community. Many of the Las Vegas elite lived in this neighborhood, where the houses sold anywhere from $1 million to $20 million. Scott continued, "He and his girlfriend moved into a condo over the weekend."

I was sick. Now I had seen lots of developers lose everything. Once the recession got into full swing, there was no escape for the developers who had large commercial projects. Either projects never got finished because banks pulled the funding, or in some cases, after the project was complete, there were no tenants to lease the property to. In either situation, the banks came knocking. But the banks didn't stop at just taking back the projects. The banks collected on all the personal guarantees. Those include all of the assets—houses, cars, jewelry. And if developers were fortunate enough to have any kind of cash left over, the banks took that as well. Many developers had fallen. But David was the first broker in our office to lose it all. That made it real.

I envisioned me and my family packing up boxes at our comfortable home and moving into an apartment. My head started to spin as I could picture my kids having to say goodbye to our neighbors and their own bedrooms, let alone the swimming pool and the sport court. My role of provider would be stripped away. And the way Skye and I were getting along, my kids might just have to say goodbye to me. I was beginning to bring my work stress home and my marriage had glided straight into rocky territory. This thought chilled me to the bone.

More than anything, I wanted to have a family that looked nothing like the one in which I was raised. If Skye and I divorced, it would be the end of the storybook life that I had dreamed of. Would she remarry? If she did, what kind of man would end up raising my boys? Would they have the same luck I had had with my stepfather? The thought made me sick.

The origins of my birth made paternal figures hard to come by. Pap was in jail, and though I'd get to visit him, there are only so many bonding moments a grandfather can have with his grandson in prison. My gram was the supreme matriarch, and my young mother briefly attempted the dual roles of mom and dad. I was a toddler and needed a father. My mom needed a partner who would appreciate her and love her. When she turned 21, she started going to bars to find such a partner.

That's where she met Jim. At 21, she married him, and he became my "official" stepdad. Jim was in his mid-thirties, a good 15 years older than my mom. He was tall, lean, and good-looking. I was so excited to have a dad. I was seven years old and had visions of playing catch in the front yard and talking about "guy" stuff. My mom was happy, smiling, and in love. I liked seeing my mom happy. Jim seemed nice at first. But then again, I didn't have much to compare him to.

The honeymoon phase didn't last long. Jim soon showed his true colors: He was a younger, angrier version of my grandfather. (I'm sure psychologists would love to take a crack at that one. Perhaps, that's why she was drawn to him. Who knows?) I learned quickly my first chance at having a real dad was a sham—an abusive, wife-beating, alcoholic sham.

One day, a family friend dropped mom, Jim, and I off at the house after grocery shopping. Jim asked me to help carry the bags in, and I obliged.

"Don't go eating this stuff," he said sternly. I sighed. What good were groceries if we couldn't eat them? As I carefully carried the bag into the house, my eyes caught the bright yellow hue of a banana bunch. The bananas looked so ripe and delicious, and I was hungry. I quickly glanced behind me to make sure no one was looking and snapped one banana off the bunch.

I plopped the bag on the kitchen table and darted out to the back yard. We had a big tree back there, which made the perfect hiding place. I plopped down on the ground behind the tree and carefully peeled my stolen banana. Just as I was about to take my second bite, I felt someone grab the collar of my shirt.

"I told you not to eat the stuff!" Jim yelled as he ripped the banana from my hand and shoved it into my face. I couldn't breathe: His huge hand covered my nose and mouth while he mashed the banana hard into my face. My nose throbbed, and I struggled to breathe. I thought he was going to kill me. He eventually pushed me to the ground and walked away, leaving me there struggling to catch my breath with banana smeared all over my face.

Thanks, "Dad."

Another time, I remember the phone ringing and my mom answering it. It was Jim calling from the bar. He needed more money, since he had drunk all his money away and was apparently still thirsty. From what I could gather from the one side of the conversation I could hear, Jim had given my mom money earlier that day for groceries. Now he wanted that money back so he could continue to drink. My mom screamed into the phone with vibrant and colorful language that she was not going to give it back. She was going to buy groceries with it and that was that. She hung up.

The very next thing I remember is Mom and me on our knees next to the front door. "Be quiet," she told me. She was clutching a baseball bat. I remember seeing Jim's white painter's pants step through the door and then hearing a smack and then Jim screeching in pain. My mom had swung the bat as hard as she could and connected with both of Jim's shins. I remember watching him crumple into a heap on the floor as my mom grabbed my hand and we ran. Jim didn't follow us. As we ran down the street, my mom began to laugh as hard as I had ever heard her laugh in my life. I guess it was the fear of what she knew was coming her way the next time she went home—or maybe she had dreamt of doing that for so long and was giddy with finally having done it. Either way, I loved that laugh and still do.

The closest *Field of Dreams* moment came when Jim took me out "shopping" for a bike. My friend, Jason, had gotten a new bike that week and I had been asking for one every single day since. "No," was the answer I got from my mom over and over again. After more crying and then giving me a beating so that I actually "had something to cry about," Jim told me to get my coat and come with him. The sky was dark that Sunday night. It must have been a Sunday because Jim was sober or as close to sober as he could get.

Jim and I walked down our hill and up another hill about three miles, to Curtin Street, a large street with big old Victorian houses built in the heyday of Bellefonte. They now housed all the rich people: Two doctors that practiced in Bellefonte, the dentist, the lawyers, and the judges. In fact, the judge who had presided over my pap's trial lived in this neighborhood.

Jim loved walking this neighborhood at night. The pickings were prime—rich people didn't protect their things like poor people did. They left their things out in the open and unlocked. As we walked quietly down the street, Jim stopped me. He had spotted a bike that was left beside the sidewalk.

"Ok, go get it and ride it over to that patch of trees," he said. "I'll meet you by the trees away from the streetlights."

I protested. "But..."

"'But nothing. Just walk up to that bike that has been thrown on its side and left for the taking. Clearly, whoever owned that bike couldn't have wanted it that badly or they would have taken better care of it."

I glanced over at the bike and back at Jim.

"Besides, all these people are rich. They can just go buy another bike," he said.

I thought about that as I walked over. My heart was pounding in my chest like a collegiate drum line. I thought it was going to burst through my ribs and fly out of my skin. When I reached the bike, I took a quick look around and grabbed the handlebars with all the strength I could muster. I pulled the bike upright and ran as fast as I could, getting the bike up to 50 mph, or at least it felt like I was running that fast when I jumped on it to pedal as fast as I could.

I was pedaling at rapid speed but nothing was happening. The chain was "popped"—it had come off the sprocket, and no matter how fast I pedaled, nothing was happening. Jim saw what was going on and started waving his arm frantically, whisper-yelling to throw the bike down and run. But I couldn't. I kept pedaling and tried to go faster. I had come this far and really wanted this bike. I was not about to throw it down and go home empty-handed.

Jim's agitation persisted. He waved his arms with more vigor and the whisper-yelling turned into full-blown swearing at the top of his lungs. "Drop that blankety-blankety bike!" he screamed for the entire neighborhood to hear. I regretfully threw it down and ran to Jim. I was met with a smack to the back of the head.

"You idiot," he screamed. It was a long walk home with him being mad and no bike to show for it. The only thing that saved me was that someone had left their car unlocked and Jim collected the contents. The haul included a lady's coat and a few bucks in the ashtray. His new find put him in a better mood. My mom would like the coat and Jim now had enough money for his first round at the bar tomorrow.

This was not the last time Jim took me stealing with him. One time we went to a grocery store and Jim started sticking anything he could in his pockets and pants. He was not very cautious about it either. Jim was in the process of shoving a ring of bologna into his pants when a lady turned and walked into the aisle. She simply turned around and went to a different aisle. Jim looked like he had gained 100 pounds, and he had developed a limp by the time we were walking out of the store. He was literally hugging himself and dragging his one leg to prevent things from falling out of his clothes.

As I am sure you have gathered by now, Jim was not the best role model. He went on another stealing spree that I did not personally witness but it lives in infamy in our family lore. One day, my gram was shopping at a store and had a few new outfits in her cart. Jim walked around the corner and saw her. Jim looked in the cart and grabbed the outfits. "I'll get those for you, Gloria," he told her.

My gram protested as much as she could, but he walked away with the outfits in hand. Gram looked at my Aunt Roseann and said, "Get me out of here." Jim's reputation was widely known throughout our family, and Gram knew he was not going to pay for the clothes. She was right. A little while later, Jim was at Gram's house with the new clothes in hand. No bag. No receipt. Just the clothes balled up as if they were shoved in someone's pants leg. Gram took them, thanked Jim, smiled, but never wore them. Instead, she gave the outfits to one of my aunts. She wanted nothing to do with Jim's thievery.

Jim would get Gram gifts when he made her mad. She came to our house one day and Jim was drunk (big surprise). Gram was upset and when she was upset, she would tell you her opinion without being asked. Jim told her, in no uncertain terms, that he didn't want her opinion and told her to get out of his house. Once Jim sobered up, he must have realized my gram was not someone you wanted on your bad side. A few mornings later, my gram discovered some gently used porch furniture on her front porch. He had taken it off of someone's porch who thought you didn't need to lock up your porch furniture. If they wanted it, they would have locked it up, he said. That was how Jim thought the world worked.

To make matters worse, Jim had taken my gram's old furniture for our own house. She had no choice but to use the furniture Jim had stolen for her. This was the worst "gift" my gram ever got. She broke out into a cold sweat every time a cop drove down her dead-end street. She would tell us all the time that she didn't know where he got it and she didn't ask, just in case. Gram went as far as putting blankets that she'd crocheted over the furniture to make it less likely that the cops would recognize it.

My Uncle Bub had a ball with this situation: Each time a cop would come down our street he would say in a loud voice, "I love your new furniture, Mom. Where did you get it?" My gram would almost die of fear.

For me, well, I was not above taking what I wanted at that stage of my life. I never did get that bike that Jim and I went "shopping" for, but later that summer I took Jon Emel's bike and hid it in my gram's basement. I have no idea what I was thinking. Jon was my best friend and lived four houses away from Gram. There was no way I would ever be able to ride that bike without him seeing it. But I didn't have to worry. Somehow his dad found out and came to my gram's house. I remember him going down to the basement and bringing the bike up the stairs while I sat there and watched. I can't remember if I came up with a story or not about how that bike got into the basement, but I can remember feeling ashamed as Jon and his dad gave me an icy stare while retrieving the stolen bike.

Jon's family had fed me and taken me with them when they went on trips to visit their family. And still, I stole from them. That shame hurts me still to this day as I document my transgression. I am not sure if that was the last time I stole, but I am pretty sure it was the last time I stole from someone I knew. I am happy that I broke that habit early on in my life by having good friends who set me straight.

Just because you're used to doing something a certain way, doesn't mean that you have to continue to do those things. This especially applies to things that you know are not right or that do not bring you joy. I honestly do not know where my life would have taken me if I did not finally learn the lesson "do not steal." I mean, it was all around me—Jim, my mom, other family members. I knew no different until—well, until I did know different.

I realized stealing wasn't the right thing to do through my group of good friends outside of the friends and family I was associated with in Coleville. These special friends gave me an important, essential self-development tool: Contrast. Many times in our lives, we will continue to do the things we've always done because we have nothing to contrast those behaviors with.

Contrast can help you in many areas of life. It sure has helped me in many areas of mine. My friends in middle school showed me the contrast between being honest and being a thief. I also credit the Weaver family for serving as a good example in my life. They showed me what a "real" family looked and sounded like. Little did I know that other families did not scream and curse at each other on a daily basis. I met them through Megan Weaver, a girl I dated in school. I found it so odd that Megan's dad did not come home drunk every day after work. I never heard him swear at his wife, Noreen, or either of their kids. To be fair, I did see him get irritated with them, but I never saw him hit them when he was mad. I remember thinking to myself, *This is the kind of family I want someday.* I wanted a family where my wife and kids would not be afraid of me. Where they would not live in fear of being beaten.

I eventually noticed a lot of contrast between what I thought was normal and what actually was normal. I saw the contrast between people who drank excessive amounts of alcohol and those who didn't drink, or just had one or two beers at a time. There was the contrast between people who did drugs and people who didn't do drugs. And the contrast between people who went to work every single day and those who only worked when they had to or didn't work at all, living off the state by choice. I saw the contrast of people who did their best in school and those who barely put forth an effort. The contrast between people who put forth 100 percent of their effort in everything that they did and those who did just enough to get by.

Seeing this contrast has helped me to make educated choices.

But there are some people who have never seen what a dysfunctional family looks like. When it comes to their own choices, they lack the contrast that I had the privilege of experiencing. People outside of the Unlucky Sperm Club may not know what it looks like to have an alcoholic in the family. Therefore, when faced with the choice, they may lack the perspective that contrast could give them, one that will help them to make an educational decision on how to consume alcohol.

That was the great thing about being a part of the Unlucky Sperm Club. I had seen contrast in almost every situation life presented me by the time I reached my early twenties. This gave me a huge advantage when choices came my way. I was able to draw upon those contrasts and make choices that led me in the direction I wanted my life to go.

I look back on that moment when my mom went all Babe Ruth on Jim. I see now that she had a strong *why*. She was not going to let him drink all the money for groceries away. She had had enough, no matter the cost.

If our *why* is big enough and strong enough, there is nothing we can't do or won't do to make it happen. As I set my goals today, I always start with my *why*. Why do I want to accomplish this goal? If I don't have a strong *why*, I don't even bother with the goal. I do this for two reasons. First, if my *why* is weak, chances are I won't accomplish the goal anyway. Second, if I don't have a strong *why*, then it is probably not my goal. It is someone else's goal or the world's goal or a goal I think someone else would be impressed with. Goals are grand, but we need to accomplish them to make a positive difference in our lives. Setting goals that you never accomplish can be demoralizing. After all, we don't want to get to a point where we don't set goals because we never achieve them.

My goals the day I found out about the terrible things David had just been through were simple: survive another day.

Chapter 9

Can Fred Come Out to Play?

"Every morning, we get a chance to be different. A chance to change. A chance to be better."

— Alan Bonner

It is somewhat ironic that a huge portion of my business investments was related to caregiving industries. If I had a therapist, I am sure they would say I was drawn to the doggie and children's day care industries because of the lack of nurturing that I received in my childhood. Some of that may be true, but at the time, I thought I just wanted to make money.

Was that why I was so blind? Did I choose money over the safety and security of the kids? Did I listen to whispers of the greed and arrogance in my personality when I made the decision to hire this man instead of the voice of reason and security? Was I really concerned with safety or concerned with money and prosperity? I told myself a thousand times not to hire a man. But I did it anyway. I went against that voice in my head and took the easier route. I ignored the sick feeling in my stomach as I shook his hand that first time to tell him that he was hired. I was not blind, I knew the risk, I was just in a hurry. As I turned on the TV, I saw the news reporting on the child molester from Bright Child once again.

That fight of morality was going on in my head as I remembered the fights I had experienced as a child.

Mom and Jim had real fights. They would throw stuff and hit each other. As I got older, I tried to protect her as best as I could, and she me, but alcoholic Jim was a force to be reckoned with. When he was sober, he wasn't all that bad to be around. But Jim was rarely sober. He drank like he would die if he didn't get enough booze into his system. It was as if he was trying to drown "sober Jim" before he could show up and be reasonable. Jim was a monster when he was drunk. He didn't care about anyone or anything. Drunk Jim had two purposes: to hurt and to humiliate.

My gram and Aunt Jane called social services on Jim and my mom because of the abuse. To this day, Aunt Jane and Mom still feud over that. Gram was always trying to get me to come and stay with her. The abuse was bad enough that I'd show up with bruises. She'd call the state and tell them I was being abused. The state would send an inspector out to the house and Jim would lie to them. Most of the time, he slurred and swore at the case worker. I would lie right alongside him, telling the case worker that Jim never hit me or my mom. (Jim had told me that if I told them he was hitting me, they would take me away. He said I would never see my mom again. I didn't want to leave my mom alone with him, and I *knew* they would take me away if they knew even a fraction of what Jim did to us on a daily basis.)

We moved a lot too. We would either get evicted for not paying the rent or because of the constant fighting at 3:00 in the morning after the bars closed. That's when Jim would get home and do what he did best. Many of the houses were homes converted into duplexes or triplexes, so we always had neighbors on either side of our walls. They would call the police as soon as the yelling and screaming started. My mom would pack our things up and we'd find another house to rent. I think I lived in eight different houses before I turned 12.

I had always wondered why my mother liked Jim, or for that matter, why my gram had married Pap. It blew me away that these two good women would ever fall for such men and then stay with them.

I remember visiting Pap in prison. The prison was about an hour away from our home, and without exception, my gram visited my pap every month. It usually wasn't just my gram either. It was often a carload of people who went with Gram, and a lot of times, I went along too. My pap was a nice guy, in person. Everyone laughed and played cards, and he was kind to everybody. But at the same time, I remembered the horrible stories that people told me about him and the horrible things that I knew he had done earlier in life. How could this friendly guy be the same horrible monster that had done terrible things that had put him behind bars? It was so confusing to me.

But it was the same thing with Jim. Granted, I got to see the evil side of him in spades. Yet I also remember times, usually on Sundays, when the bars were closed and Jim showed a side of himself that wasn't completely evil. I think that a lot of my mom and Jim's issues, and Jim's meanness, had to do with the heavy drinking. Pap and Jim had to be decent men, at some point in their lives, to attract such good women. I recall people telling me good stories about these guys. But at some point they chose, whether with the assistance of alcohol or not, to be evil people.

I believe that all of us have two people living inside of us, one that wants to do the right thing and one that wants to do the wrong thing. It's up to us which one of those people gets to make the choices for us. It's like those cartoons in which there's a devil on someone's shoulder and an angel on the other. The angel is always trying to get someone to do the right thing, while the devil tries to get him to do the wrong thing.

I think this concept is best described in an old Cherokee teaching: A man is teaching his grandson about life. "A fight is going on inside of me," he said to the boy. "It's a terrible fight between two wolves. One is evil. He is anger, envy, sorrow, regret, greed, arrogance, self-pity, guilt, resentment, inferiority, lies, false pride, superiority, and ego. The other is good. He is joy, peace, love, hope, serenity, humanity, kindness, benevolence, empathy, generosity, truth, compassion, and faith. The same fight is going on inside of you and inside of every other person." He looked to the grandson, who thought about it for a minute.

The grandson asked his grandfather, "Which wolf will win?"

The old Cherokee simply replied, "The one you feed."

I think this was the case in my grandfather's and in Jim's lives. At one time, they were both decent men, but they started to feed their bad wolves through simple steps, each and every day. I think it's the same for all of us: Throughout our days and our years, we feed one of these two wolves, and the one that wins is the one that we feed the most. We must be careful not to feed the bad wolf too much, or too often, because before we know it, that bad wolf will get bigger and stronger and he will take over. Feed that good wolf—feed the joy, the love, the kindness. Have empathy and practice generosity, be truthful and compassionate, and have faith. Let that good wolf win and let him help you in your decisions in your life.

I use this technique in my life each day. I have an alter ego. His name is Fred, and Fred always makes the right choices. Fred has the distinction of being Father of the Year, as well as the Husband of the Year. He always stays focused and he never gives up. He's perfect in every way. Fred would never dream of eating chocolate cake if he were on a diet. He'd never dream of yelling at the kids when it's his goal to stay calm. He'd never dream of not finishing his to-do list before the end of the day or skipping his daily workout by sleeping in. Fred always thanks his wife for everything that she does, and he's always encouraging and supportive to his kids. He looks for opportunities to spend time with them. If they're playing video games when he gets home, he asks them to go outside and play ball. Fred would never take an opportunity to sit on the couch and mindlessly watch TV.

Fred is full of love, compassion, and empathy. He always looks for what he can do to help. He's very slow to anger and can't be irritated, and he loves doing the right thing.

And then there's *Nelson*. If *he* comes home and finds that the kids are upstairs and playing video games, he might just slip onto the couch and turn on the TV and veg for as long as his wife will let him. If there was chocolate cake in the kitchen, Nelson would surely sneak a bite—and then another—and then another. And Nelson has no problem staying in bed and skipping a workout, if he gets an opportunity.

Whenever questions or decisions come up, I always ask Fred's advice on what to do. Of course, Fred always picks the *right* thing to do. The more I take Fred's advice, the more Nelson starts to see the benefit of making Fred-type choices—and the less I have to ask Fred's advice because Nelson starts to make the same choices that Fred would make. It's less about a split personality than it is about acknowledging my innate ability to be both Fred and Nelson, even though my wife does say I am a little cray cray.

This is a great technique for us because we're human and our brains are wired to do the easy things to keep us out of danger and to avoid discomfort. We need to push ourselves into situations that make us uncomfortable because that's the only place we'll grow and the only place that we'll get better.

We all have a Fred inside of us who is perfect and makes the right decisions. Find your Fred. Give him a name and ask his opinion whenever those choices come up. Have him help to guide your choices and your decisions. What the wise old Cherokee said is very true. The wolf that's going to win is the one that's fed the most!

Start feeding the right wolf and making the right choices, and watch how things fall into place more regularly and more naturally. It becomes easier and you will become much more like the alter ego, the good wolf. I have found this to be true as I strive to be more like Fred.

My kids and my wife joke with me whenever Nelson has an outburst or shows signs of irritation. "Can Fred come out to play, please?" they ask. This is a great indicator to me that I am not making the choices that are going to make me a better person and that I should go back to asking Fred for his advice.

Knowing who we do not want to be is just as important as telling ourselves who we want to be. I was positive that I never wanted to be like Pap or like Jim. Growing up in Pennsylvania, I really didn't know what I wanted to do in life, but I knew what I *didn't* want to do. I knew who I *didn't* want to be. I knew how I *didn't* want to act, and I knew the things that I *didn't* want to ever do, not under any circumstances. Sometimes that's good enough. Sometimes we don't have a clear picture of who we want to be or what we want to do, but we have a picture of who we *don't* want to be. We know the things that we don't want to do. We can work at getting as far away from those things that we don't want to do or be. We can put as much distance between ourselves and those things as possible.

As a kid, I didn't have strong role models whom I could point to in life, but I knew what I didn't want to be. I read books about people who had succeeded and how they had stood on the shoulders of giants. These great people pay homage to those who had come before them and showed them the way to be successful. By following the example of those great people that came before them, these people were able to do even better and more impressive things than their predecessors.

Well, I knew that I had the opportunity to stand on the shoulders of giants. However, those giants were giant losers. If you don't have a clear vision of where you want to be or who you want to be, just get away from what you *don't* want to be and you'll see a bigger, broader perspective. This will allow you to step back, take a breath, and assess the whole scenario and how you want to fit into it. You will then be able to focus on who you *do* want to be and what you *do* want to become. And the nice thing is, you can always do this exercise any time in life when you need to gain a better perspective or realign your priorities or set new goals. It will always bring renewed clarity and definitive perspective.

I worked hard not to end up like Jim, having to dig through the trash to provide for my family and beating up the people I was supposed to love. I knew what I didn't want my life to be like.

But now, watching the news cover Bright Child over and over even as I searched for clarity and perspective, I needed some giant shoulders to stand on to see my way out of this mess. I wasn't sure there were shoulders tall enough to show me my way forward, but I had to try.

Chapter 10

Standing Up to Fear

"In the game of life, it's a good idea to have a few early losses, which relieves you of the pressure of trying to maintain an unde-feated season."

— Bill Vaughan

It is hard to pinpoint the first time I got genuinely nervous about the commercial real estate climate. Maybe it was when the banks started denying everyone loans no matter how good their credit. Or it could have been when I saw David's Nissan Maxima replace his Mercedes. I tried to keep my fear to myself, but it eventually made its way into my home and into my already-struggling marriage.

I thought I would not let this uncontrollable circumstance control me. I would not let the economic downturn make me feel weak or fearful. Instead, I continued to plod along, searching for deals and trying to resuscitate the ones I already had and trying to save my businesses and my home life. I had to keep control of the things I could control. That was the only way that I felt like anything that I did mattered in this situation. *I am in control,* I kept telling myself.

But was I really?

When I was 11, I looked fear in the face with my jaw clenched and my eyes open wide. It was the first time I'd had to overcome fear, and I did it by realizing that I was truly the one in control. As I sat in front of the TV watching Bright Child get skewered, I remembered this moment, and I immediately felt my jaw tighten with resolve just as it had that day when I was 11.

It was a typical day at our house: Jim had come home drunk and angry over something. He was always looking for somebody to take it out on. Truthfully, I'm not sure what the reason was that day, but I was his prey. And I knew it. When he picked me, I was relieved it wasn't going to be my mom.

The assault started like it normally did, with Jim stalking through the house like a caged animal and growling at everyone he saw. I knew it was only a matter of seconds before he'd charge me, just like a bear, and grab me by the arm, lifting me in the air and taking aim with his fist. But something in me snapped. I was sick of being scared of the beatings and sick of being afraid of him. I knew what was coming. I knew the pain. I knew the look. Bloodshot eyes and hate in every slurred word spewing out of his mouth as he told me in a hundred different ways how horrible I was. But I was done giving him what I knew he wanted.

That day, I wasn't scared of what was coming. A kind of peace washed over me. Whatever he did, I could take it. I had been through it enough times before and always survived. Instead of running and hiding like I normally did, I just stood there, waiting. Jim staggered across the room toward me. As he got closer, I didn't flinch. He grabbed me by the wrist and lifted me in the air so that my toes barely touched the floor.

Jim whacked my butt, or as close as he could get in his drunken state. *Smack. Smack. Thud.* Many of the blows hit me in the small of the back or my thighs, but he had a lot of practice, so a good number of them hit their target. I would not give him the satisfaction of crying this time. I remember taking the first five or six blows and feeling the pain radiate through my body. Normally, I would be screaming at the top of my lungs, hoping that he thought he was killing me. When I did that he normally stopped because he got the reaction that he wanted. Not this time.

Jim dished out another five or six blows until he came to realize that there was something different. No scream had escaped my lips. The pain was there but I wasn't affected by it. The will to mentally beat Jim was the only way I could muster my strength and take the beating until his arm fell off. He took a few more swings at me and then he stopped. Slowly, he lowered me back onto the floor. I could tell he was confused because he wasn't saying anything. I don't know if he thought he had really injured me or what was going through his mind, but he knew this was not normal.

I will never forget his face when I turned around to look at him. He gazed back at me with confusion and, I'd like to think, fear.

"Go to your room and don't come out," he said, with much less confidence than his previous post-beating statements. Normally he would scream this command at me. I'd run before he changed his mind. This time, I walked slowly, with my teeth clenched so tight my jaw hurt. I walked up the steps slowly and deliberately with as much satisfaction as I could muster. An 11-year-old boy just beat Jim at the one thing that he was good at. He was no longer undefeated.

As I crossed the threshold into my room, I quietly shut the door and then collapsed in a fit of tears. I think that they were the sweetest tears ever cried. They were tears of winning the battle and knowing that no matter what, if I was strong enough, I was in control. I couldn't control what he did to me, but I could control how I reacted to it. Best of all, Jim now knew that too.

Watching the financial market crumble before my eyes in the chaotic world of commercial real estate in 2008 was like that first showdown.

This time, too, I wanted to run away and cry, even scream so loud that the universe could hear me and think that it was killing me and the rest of the world and have some compassion and stop all the ugly things that were happening, but I didn't. At least, not loud enough to change things.

The next few months were a roller coaster. Deal after deal fell out of escrow and my clients lost millions of dollars. I lost the fees that were to be paid to me when these deals closed. Many of these properties that were in escrow to be sold were headed to foreclosure. The properties quickly lost tenants who were paying the rent. It was the perfect storm against a commercial real estate broker because nothing was selling. There were no buyers, nobody was leasing, and nobody had any money. If nobody was buying or leasing, then brokers were not making any money on fees.

This is when I decided to forget about the things that I could not control, like the wind. I had to start focusing on the things that I could control, like the sail of my ship.

Chapter 11

In the Weeds

"Don't water your weeds."

— **Proverb**

By now, I had invested a lot of my own money in my business ventures. I had the lovely high-interest loan to complete the Sweet Pea building I developed, which was at last completed and open. But there was a new problem, as if things weren't bad enough.

As 2008 rolled into 2009 and then 2010, people didn't need day care as badly as they did in the years prior to the crisis. Supply far outweighed demand these days when it came to day care centers. This issue was twofold: People in Las Vegas didn't have enough money to pay for day care because many of them had lost jobs. The blue-collar workers were impacted the most. The hardworking construction workers suddenly had no construction projects and thus, no income. The hospitality employees who worked on the Las Vegas Strip soon lost their jobs or had their hours drastically cut and needed to find a way to make ends meet. Home-based day cares started popping up all over Las Vegas. These day cares charged a fraction of what we charged. I can't blame them—they were doing anything they could to survive.

However, this increase in competition made it almost impossible for Sweet Pea to survive. We were hemorrhaging clients. The checks from Sweet Pea had stopped a year earlier, which sucked. But when the owner came to me and my father-in-law asking for money to float the businesses, it *really* sucked. I was feeding Doggie District and the commercial properties that were in the red each month. I had almost no money coming in through my commercial brokerage business and now I was going to be feeding Sweet Pea. Years earlier, I had read the book *Multiple Streams of Income*. I had patterned my investments following that book. I had dreamed of many income streams flowing right into my bank account. This was when I realized my dyslexia was kicking in: I must have read that book backwards, since all my multiple streams of income were going in reverse.

My father-in-law was not in much better shape than I was. He was battling kidney failure and would soon need a transplant. He'd be forced to quit practicing dentistry in short order. And he had invested his life savings into these day cares. As enrollments dropped and the checks ceased, I started to get a little nervous. After all, it was me who got him into this investment. I couldn't predict this would happen, but I sure felt guilty about it. We were not only not getting checks, we were going to have to write checks to keep the business going. It was a double whammy for both of us.

Naturally I brought that guilt home, and that led to more fights with Skye creating a perfect storm of uncertainty and resentment. Real estate deals were few and far between. I was starting to have trouble meeting the needs of my immediate family financially.

My father-in-law and I decided that we would fund the Sweet Pea centers but we had one condition. To drum up some business and raise awareness of Sweet Pea, we decided we needed to hire someone to do some marketing. At first, the owner of Sweet Pea protested, saying we didn't have the money to hire someone. I agreed we didn't have the money, but I was convinced that we were going to die a slow death if we didn't change things and try and get a bigger piece of the ever-shrinking day care pie. We hired a woman to visit the centers and determine the best way to increase our enrollment in the midst of a crumbling economy. What set Sweet Pea apart? What did Sweet Pea offer that other day cares did not?

The answers were worse than we could have imagined.

Our marketing hire found out that our operating partner in Sweet Pea was a complete shyster. He was running a horrible operation. No wonder he hadn't wanted us to hire a sharp-eyed consultant! He had the centers literally plop kids down into chairs with a fistful of crayons and paper towels to draw on. Paper towels, not paper! They weren't even white paper towels; they were brown. I could just imagine a sweet child taking their artwork home drawn on a brown paper towel: "Look what I did today, Mommy!"

This guy had no shame. We had recently given him $350,000 to fund the starting of the new center I had just completed construction on. It turns out, all he did was to close down a center that he had owned before we had become partners and moved the 15-year-old furniture, fixtures, and equipment from it to the brand-new day care center we were partners on. He pocketed the entire $350,000.

The more we dug, the more snakes we found. This guy was paying his daughters hundreds of thousands of dollars through the day cares to do absolutely nothing. He paid all of his bills through the day care centers: His house payment, the landscaper for his house, his pool guy…everything. We were supposed to be partners on these ventures, but we had partnered with a master embezzler.

My father-in-law and I had been happy with our checks. We had no idea this was going on until we explored our marketing options. Our consultant determined the day cares were going to go belly up, and soon.

"You're going to lose your investments," she said somberly.

I was going to lose more than that. I was going to lose my marriage. I had already lost tons of money. I was going to lose my other investments. Not only was I going to lose everything, my father-in-law was going to lose everything he had worked for his entire life, just as he was being forced into retirement because of his kidney issues.

I had followed a snake into the weeds and taken my family with me.

Growing up, I had learned about the dangers of going into the weeds the hard way. I knew there was no way of coming out unscathed. And here I was, neck-high and lost.

Coleville, the place where we lived with Gram and most of her kids, was an old mining town. Warner Company, the owner of the mine, had two huge gypsum mines in our area. One was just east of Coleville and you could see the two stacks of steam that billowed out from the top every single day. The other one was about five miles to the west of Coleville. It was called the Gyp. I'm guessing because of the gypsum that it produced. Warner owned all the land between the two plants. They had built 20 or 30 houses in the early 1900s to house the plant workers. Eventually, they sold off the houses to people who didn't work at the plant. One of those houses was Gram's. She and Pap paid $1,500 for the house. And most of the other houses were occupied by my aunts and uncles.

The good thing about growing up in Coleville was you had all of this land that the mine owned to explore and play on. The company didn't care much about what went on above ground. They were only concerned with what they were bringing out of the ground. So they left us alone to explore and play on the land. Another good thing was that the mine had built a park 50 years earlier. It was only a quarter-mile from my grandma's house. We affectionately called this park "the ball field," even though there was more than just a baseball park on it. It had a full-fledged baseball diamond with 30-foot high concrete bleachers. The concrete was chipped and worn, but the bleachers still served a purpose. In right field, the company paved an area and put up a basketball court. Scattered around the park sat some dilapidated playground equipment. Of course, no one maintained it so the weeds and the grass grew tall on the baseball field.

That is, until my Uncle Ralph got it in his mind to mow the field, restoring it to playing condition. In between my Uncle Ralph's voluntary maintenance, the grass grew to three or four feet tall. It had to be mowed several times until it was playable. Then Uncle Ralph would find an old set of metal box springs from the junkyard down the street and hook it to the back of his truck. He would tell three or four kids to get on top of the box springs and then drag the box springs around the infield. This process would remove all the grass, weeds, and large rocks, trapping them in the box spring.

Ralph had a weird sense of humor: Whenever three or four kids were on those box springs, he would hit the gas, turn the wheel really sharp, and whip us around. He knew exactly when to hit the gas and when to turn the wheel to make us go 30 or 40 miles an hour. If we were lucky, we would just roll off through the grass, getting small scrapes and cuts. Often, the box springs would hit something on its edge and the entire set of box springs would roll with us kids on it, leaving us with more cuts and scrapes. The men working on the field would have tears coming out of their eyes from laughing so hard as us kids screamed for Ralph to stop. Most of us knew what was coming when Ralph started his "Spin of Death" routine. We'd jump off and take our chance in the fields, rolling five or six times at what felt like a hundred miles an hour before our bodies came to a complete stop. The other kids who were too afraid to jump just hung on as tight as they could. At least those kids had a chance that Ralph would come to his senses and realize that someone could really get hurt at the speed he was going.

After Ralph and the rest of the guys got the field ready for play, they would schedule a softball game. This was a huge to-do in Coleville, and it was much like any other party that my family had. Of course, there was a keg of beer or two for the men. And every family in attendance would bring their covered dish.

Just like every Fourth of July, once the beer was gone there would be a fight. Aunt Sue would lift the keg to see if it would float on the melted ice. When she packed up to leave, we knew it was fight time. Aunt Sue was more frightened of the fights that happened at the softball fields then the Fourth of July parties. The softball fields had baseball bats, and when they made an appearance in a fight, there were always three or four people who had to go to the ER. (The Fourth of July parties had horseshoes that were thrown at people's heads, but fortunately they never connected.)

We kids were never allowed to play in the real softball game, but once the fight was over and the game was over, the field was left to us. We would play baseball, Wiffle ball, or football on the field.

The field was in really nice condition, but on both sides of the field where they didn't cut the grass, there grew "the weeds." The weeds were anywhere from three to six feet tall depending on the year. If the adults hit a ball into the weeds, they just left it there. The ball was not worth going into the "the weeds" to get it. But we kids couldn't afford to lose a ball to the weeds. If a ball landed in the jungle, we'd go in after it. In fact, we were able to recover the balls the adults left out there and use them for future games. Balls were expensive.

The expedition came with risks. There was no doubt you'd come out of the weeds with some issues. Best-case scenario was poison ivy or scratching from the nettles. (If you're not familiar with what "nettles" are, imagine pouring gasoline on your arm, lighting it, and then grabbing an electric fence.) Worst-case scenario was if you got into "jagger bushes." If this was the case, you would have jaggers all over your body. There was no getting these jaggers off your clothes without picking out each individual burr. And when you came out of the weeds it wasn't like you only had five or 10 of these jaggers on you. No, you had thousands.

The worst was if you got jaggers in your hair. If that happened, you knew you were in for a long night. I remember going home to my gram's one time with a bunch of jaggers in my hair. She didn't even try to comb them out with water like she usually did. She just grabbed a pair of scissors and started cutting. She must've had a bad day. But truthfully it was better to just have them cut out than extracted with a comb and water. If she tried to pull them out, it hurt. She would comb it out with a comb and pull with all her strength, and all you would hear was her telling you, "How many times have I told you to stay out of the weeds?"

The funny thing was, these were not usually the worst haircuts my grandma gave me. If you remember what the little Dutch boy on the paint cans looked like, with hair down past his ears and cut straight across his forehead. you've got Gram's go-to haircut. She would cut across your bangs in a jagged line. Gram would make five or six cuts, and none of those cuts lined up with any of the others.

As we go throughout our lives, we have all kinds of chances to go into "the weeds." I've worked with people who have gone into the weeds in business and did not make it out without being covered in their own "jaggers." During the ramp-up of the subprime mortgage boom in the early and mid-2000s, a guy I knew came up with a scam with a few of his working partners to sell homes for way more than they were really worth (even during the boom). This scheme had a real estate appraiser, an attorney, and a residential real estate broker. They would get people who wouldn't normally qualify for a loan and promised that they could get them approved for the loan. They would add 20 percent to 50 percent over the value of the home than what it was worth. Then the three men would split the lucrative profit after the home closed. This went on for years until the crash came and all the loans that they did went bad because of all the false information they used to get people qualified for the loans. The people that they got qualified couldn't afford to pay the loans and the banks had to foreclose.

These three successful men had families and great careers. They had a good life going and decided that they were going to go into the weeds to make some big easy money. They didn't make it out. All three did time in prison, leaving their families behind. When they got out, none of them were able to practice in the industries that they did prior because they all lost their license to do so.

You don't make it out of the weeds unscathed.

I've had friends go into the weeds on their families and spouses. These people had great families, good kids, and nice homes. But they threw it all away when they decided to go into "the weeds" on their marriage. For a few nights of romance, they lost their families and ruined their marriages. These were good men. I still call them my friends. But they went into the weeds and they are now paying the consequences.

Another acquaintance of mine, a surgical assistant, decided to go into the weeds. He, along with two others, devised a scheme to sell prescription medication through one of the nurses who had access to a doctor's prescription pad. The doctor would sign the prescription pad and give it to his nurse, who gave it to the guy I knew. From there, my acquaintance would fill them out for whatever drug a customer wanted. Many times, these people who received the prescriptions were addicted to pain pills and used their Medicare or Medicaid insurance to fill the prescription. Eventually, the scheme was uncovered by the FBI, and all three people involved were arrested and are either in prison or awaiting their sentencing. The guy I knew not only lost his job and his family but he is now heading to prison for a long time. He made approximately $30,000 through the scheme. I'm not sure any of us would trade four to six years in prison for $30,000.

The weeds are all around us. There is no shortage of opportunity to go into them. Many times, when we're not paying attention, we can drift into the weeds in certain areas of our lives. Sometimes things don't seem black and white but gray. When things are gray, there are no boundaries, and many times, no lines that we know we shouldn't cross. We need to be cautious as we go throughout our days not thinking that we are above the effects of our actions. Many times, when you have this train of thought, you don't realize you're in the thick of the weeds until it's too late. By the time you realize you're deep in the weeds, there's no option but to keep going.

I have tried to live my life by sketching out some absolutes. These absolutes have guided me as I make decisions in my life. We all have different standards and values, so I will not impose my absolutes on you. However, I would suggest that you sit down and write down your absolutes. An absolute is a thing that under no circumstances you are willing to compromise.

It was very clear where the men mowed the ball field. There was no question where the field stopped and the weeds began. These absolutes will make it just as clear for you. You can have a concrete idea of where your standards and values end and what lines you don't want to cross.

If you don't have these absolutes, you might end up in the weeds and thus with a haircut not of your choosing.

Chapter 12

Nelson Nobody

"Life is for one generation, a good name is forever."

— Anonymous

Once the corruption and embezzlement came to light, we confronted the Sweet Pea owner. He, of course, denied everything but there was no question it was all true. We had bank records and employees who were willing to testify against the owner. I now had a choice to make.

I knew for certain that I was justified to sue him for all that he had embezzled from the company and possibly even bring criminal charges against him. If I pursued that option, I might get a judgment against him. Yet I was almost certain that by the time we were done not only would the day cares be out of business but the day care operator would probably be bankrupt as well. The only thing we could do was get control of the day cares and try to save our investment. Since my father-in-law and I had provided all the money to start them, the day care operator didn't have any of his own money invested in these day cares, plus he had embezzled more than $1 million over the last eight years. He would lose nothing if Sweet Pea went out of business. The centers were in the red and there was no real hope of them ever being turned around in this financial environment.

We had to do something, and we had to do it quick. He sent us a proposal. He wanted $250,000 in cash and he would walk away and turn the centers over to me and my father-in-law—$250,000! He should be in jail, not receiving a payoff for running our centers into the ground. But we had no choice: the owner was willing to let the day cares go bankrupt if we didn't pay him.

The attorneys drafted up the paperwork, and we wrote the check.

Writing a $250,000 check during the financial crisis to buy out a guy you could and should sue the pants off of is a humbling experience. I really didn't have the money to spare. I mean, who does? But my father-in-law and I shuffled a few things around and sold some other assets to come up with the money. Without that buyout, there would be no hope for my father-in-law or myself. We'd lose everything. If it were just me involved, I'd rather not throw good money after bad money. I certainly would rather not give this guy a penny, I would have walked away. But I couldn't do that to my father-in-law. Too much was at stake.

With the embezzler smugly counting dollar bills under whatever bridge he'd emerged from in the first place, I set to work on running the day care centers. The world was imploding, but it felt good to have a new cause, a new project to dive into. First things first: We changed the name. Sweet Pea had earned a horrible reputation on paper towel drawings alone. I envisioned a curriculum where kids actually learned things instead of being babysat. We came up with the name Bright Child Learning Center. It would be everything Sweet Pea was not.

Or so I hoped.

What's in a name? One Saturday morning when I was eight, Gram and my Aunt Rose Ann stopped by our house. They had just been out scouring Bellefonte for yard sales. My gram had found an awesome Philadelphia Eagles jersey that was my size. She knew I loved to play football. It was green with the number seven on it and the player's name on the back. I loved it. The following Monday I put on the jersey and walked to school, so proud to have it, just knowing that everyone at school would love it as much as I did.

No one really took notice of it until our first recess. We played football every recess, so I couldn't wait to play today with my new jersey.

I ran down to the field where the game was being played and jumped on a team. After running a few plays, a few boys who were watching started to point and laugh. At first, no one knew who they were pointing and laughing at, but eventually their group got bigger and the laughs got louder as they talked with other kids. Soon about 20 kids were pointing and laughing. They were laughing at me.

Oh no, what was it now? Then I heard the leader of the mob yelling my name. "Hey Nelson, why do you have on Brian's jersey?"

"What do you mean Brian's jersey? This is mine. My gram just got it for me," I yelled back.

"Well it must have been out of his garbage because it has his name on the back of it," he taunted. I was confused. "Look at the name on the back, you idiot. It says Larimer. That's Brian's jersey. I've seen him wear it before."

The name on the jersey wasn't the name of a professional football player who played for the Philadelphia Eagles, it was the name of a kid who was two years older than me. My gram must have bought it at his family's yard sale, and we didn't realize it was the name of a kid that went to my elementary school. I got called "Larimer" the rest of that school year.

Issues with my name didn't go away at elementary school. When I was in high school, I often met new people and introduced myself as Nelson. Simply Nelson. I tried not to say my last name because I knew exactly what would happen after I said *Tressler*. Their eyes would dart downward, their countenance would change, and seemingly out of nowhere they would suddenly have somewhere else they needed to be—if I was lucky. If not, they would ask me straight out if I was related to the guy who shot the cop and then follow that with a jittery laugh.

I never knew if they expected for me to be related or if they were asking just to be funny. But once they realized that I was not only related to Pap, but the result of the rape of the cop killer's daughter, the mood changed. A thick awkwardness always hung in the air. Neither would know how to act. Each of us would be uncertain which one of us felt more uncomfortable. There was always a sticky, clumsy, "I've got to go" or "Wow, that's crazy, I'll see you later," as we both looked at our feet and shuffled away, eager to disentangle ourselves from the embarrassing moment.

Growing up with the Tressler name elicited more than just awkward introductions. When I was in the eighth grade, our school held a formal dance. I was so excited to have an excuse to ask Megan Weaver to the dance. I'd had a crush on her for months but was afraid to talk to her. I finally had one of my friends ask her for me if she would go to the dance with me. To my surprise and horror, she said yes. I needed to figure out a way to get to the dance with Megan. Uncle Gibby and his wife, Sandy, were the only relatives who had new cars. Sandy had a new Ford Bronco II that was only a few months old. It was by far the nicest car on our street. Now who could I ask to drive me there? I couldn't ask my mom because she and Sandy didn't talk anymore. (That fight had started over cheating at the card table.) But my cousin John, Uncle Bub's son, had just gotten his driver's license. The plan was set. On the night of the dance, I rented my tux, bought a corsage, and went to pick up my date.

I knocked at Megan's door and her mother answered. I introduced myself and walked inside. They told me Megan was in her room putting on the final touches. Then Mr. Weaver walked out of the living room and introduced himself. He was very standoffish. Mrs. Weaver started some small talk that eventually led to who was driving us to the dance. I told her it was my cousin John. The already cold atmosphere turned frigid as Megan's parents looked at each other. The news was not welcome. They both said they were going to check on Megan and left me standing there as awkward as I had ever felt. Five minutes later, Megan's parents came walking back in the living room followed by Megan.

We took a few pictures and then Mrs. Weaver said that Megan had to leave half an hour early from the dance because of a family event so she'd pick her up. I said that I would leave early, too, and bring her home, but her mom said that where they were going was on the way to the dance and it was just easier for them to pick her up. I said okay and we went out to climb into the Bronco.

Mr. Weaver took more pictures of me helping her into the car than he did in their house, and that he took a few pictures of John holding the door open for us and a few of us backing out of the driveway. We made it to the dance and John dropped us off and we had a good time. Mrs. Weaver was there 30 minutes early and picked her up, and I didn't think much more about it.

Megan and I started to date after that dance, and we dated all through high school. Eventually, I got to know the Weaver family very well and spent a lot of time with them. They were my second family. I am not sure where I would have ended up if I didn't have their family during high school. A few years after we started dating, Mrs. Weaver told me what had happened the night of the eighth grade dance. They weren't going to let her go with me. They knew my family and didn't want Megan anywhere near me but Megan had insisted. But then I showed up with my male teenage cousin as our chauffeur and they were really ready to call it off. Being Tresslers, they thought we had a plan to pull over and rape her. Mrs. Weaver told me that Mr. Weaver waited for us to get out of the driveway and then got into his car and followed us to the dance to make sure nothing bad happened. She also told me that there wasn't any family event after the dance and that if Megan hadn't agreed to be picked up early, they wouldn't have let her go.

How I just wanted for my last name to be "Nobody." Life would have been so much easier if I were just "Nelson Nobody." I wouldn't have had to pay for the sins of generations before me. I would not be judged because of things that had happened before I was even born. I could stand on my own merit and be the person that I wanted to be, without prejudice or disdain.

I had a few aliases while growing up. Whenever I met people I didn't know, I threw an alias at them. One of my favorites was "Nelson Rockefeller." Not many people believed I was a Rockefeller but at least it got a laugh. Many times, the laughter was enough, and I didn't have to follow through and divulge my last name.

As I write this book, the name "Tressler" has a totally different meaning. Whenever we talk to our friends about achievements in our lives or our kids' lives, a common response back to us is, "Of course, they did, they're Tresslers." This comment doesn't have a negative connotation. In fact, it's quite the opposite. Such comments might be heard whenever our kids win an award, or if the Tresslers beat another family at bowling or in a game of cornhole, or when one of our sons makes the all-star team. In Las Vegas, the Tressler name has morphed into one of success and respect.

This could not be any further from what the name meant when I was growing up and what it still means some 3,000 miles to the east. I am very protective of my name in my professional career, as well as in our personal lives. I've been blessed with three boys who all will carry the last name of Tressler. I have stressed how my sons should protect that name, and always ensure that it has a positive meaning because they are going to have it for the rest of their lives and so will their wives and their children.

Our reputations are priceless. If one's name is synonymous with trust and respect, then he has earned that reputation and he has led a blessed and productive life.

I'm reminded of a few stories of my friends who lived their lives in a manner that made their last names synonymous with trust and respect as well. My friend, Aaron Lewis, grew up in the Moapa Valley, a small farming settlement just outside of Las Vegas. His father lived out there and he was very active in the community. He owned a construction company and did very well for himself. But that's not why his family is so well respected nor is it the reason that a park was built and named after Aaron's dad.

Every Christmas, Aaron's father loaded up his truck with 70 or so hams. With his family, he went around the Moapa Valley and delivered a ham to every widow in town. I've been with Aaron when he's introduced himself to someone and the conversation has always turned to where he's from. Aaron says he's from Moapa. Then the people ask if he knows or is related to Ron Lewis, and Aaron says, "Yeah, he was my dad," and the peoples' eyes light up and they instantly say, "Ron Lewis was one of the best people I've ever met." They then tell a story of when Ron Lewis did something so far above and beyond for them that they will never forget it. This is an example of a true legacy. We all have the opportunity for a legacy that we can pass down to future generations.

Many of us think about what we will pass down or perhaps receive in the way of an inheritance. These are usually tangible items like watches, houses, acreage, and other material things. What we should be most concerned about is passing down a legacy of doing good and of being honorable and well respected. There is nothing more valuable, and yet a price tag can never be attached to one's reputation or legacy. I try to keep this in mind as I go about my dealings in the world. I try to protect my integrity. I want to leave a legacy for my family like the one Aaron Lewis' dad left for him so that whenever there's a conversation and anyone hears the last name "Tressler," they'll instantly have a favorable impression. If anyone should ask my sons if they knew Nelson Tressler, even long after I'm gone, I want for my boys to feel pride when they answer. Better still would be if my sons might hear a story about how one time, I did the right thing, or how I once went above and beyond to help someone.

When I am put into a situation in which I have the opportunity to *not* do the best thing I can, I imagine that the people involved will someday have a conversation with my sons. How do I want that conversation to go? Do I want people to light up and tell my sons what an honorable and respected person I am or was, or do I want my sons to be told a story that will make them feel shame associated with having my last name?

If things kept going the way they were going, my last name could be all I had to pass down to my boys.

Chapter 13

Addition by Subtraction

"When things aren't adding up in your life, start subtracting."

— **Anonymous**

I now controlled the Sweet Peas. I had changed the name of all six of them to Bright Child Learning Centers and done everything I could to try to turn them around. The problem was, I had spent almost all my cash reserves buying out the Sweet Pea owner and converting and properly supplying the six centers. I didn't have any cash reserves left, and I had no real prospects of any real cash coming in anytime soon. For the fourth month in a row, I couldn't pay all the rents for the businesses. I tried to rotate which landlords and banks I paid, alternating payments every other month so that they would at least feel some hope that I was going to start paying them again on a constant basis. I wanted them to have hope that I was somehow going to make it out of this. It was in stark contrast to the hopelessness I actually felt.

Ring. Ring. Ring. It was one of the landlords calling. I knew what they were calling for—the rent. And I knew I didn't have it. The one thing I didn't know was where I was going to get it.

I had always been an optimistic guy, always looking for the bright side of every situation. Maybe after losing everything, I would happen upon something grand and awesome, something I'd have never found if I hadn't hit rock-bottom first. We have all heard those stories. This was pretty much my last hope. A hope that I would have some kind of addition in my life from the massive subtraction that was about to take place.

Ring! Ring! Ring! Oh no, another landlord…

Gram's house was always comfortable and safe. There was a routine and a sense of peace that I never felt at my house because of all the chaos there. Each night at my gram's was consistent. I would get a bath, a bowl of ice cream, and an hour of TV. Then it was time for bed. There was no screaming or fighting or drinking, and because of the peace I felt at my gram's I slept as soundly as I ever did.

Ring. Ring. Ring. I don't remember hearing the phone ring as I slept soundly on the floor next to Gram's bed. Gram woke me up.

"Jim's dead. Somebody hit him on the road," she said with the same intonation of someone commenting about the weather.

I blinked my eyes awake. *What?*

Yesterday was Jim's birthday. My mom and Jim were out drinking at The Lime Dust Inn, just a few miles away from Gram's, to celebrate. It is how they celebrated everything. Since it would certainly shape up to be a night of debauchery and libations, the kids were sent out for some good old-fashioned babysitting. My brothers and sister were being watched by one of my girl cousins.

Almost every time Mom and Jim were drinking, they would get into a huge fight. Last night had been no different. After too many drinks, they started squabbling. Fed up, my mom stormed out of the bar and walked home. A short time later, Jim left the bar as well. As he stumbled out of the bar, he made his way onto a two-way road next to a dusty lime plant. Another bar patron, who was also drunk, climbed into his vehicle and took off down the same two-way road. He hit Jim, killing him instantly.

Mom.

I wasn't sure how much time had passed since Gram woke me up. I shuffled out of my sleeping bag and rolled it up. I could hear a little bit of commotion coming from downstairs. I got dressed and plodded down to discover a few family members had heard the news and stopped by.

At first, no one knew where my mom was. There was someone sleeping on the couch covered in blankets. At Gram's that could be anyone. Usually, it was Uncle Bub. But on this fateful day, the bundled being was my mother.

My Uncle Nelson, an early riser, was out for his morning coffee when he happened upon the crews cleaning up the accident. As soon as he found out it was Jim, he called Gram. She must have made a few phone calls to try to find my mom, not knowing she was already downstairs. That explained the cavalry convened in Gram's living room. They gently woke up my mom and broke the news. She was groggy, possibly hungover, as she processed what they were saying. Then it hit her, and she fainted. It was unnerving to see.

I, on the other hand, didn't feel much grief or shock. Jim had been the only father figure I had ever had but he had been a horrible one. I never wished him dead but I wasn't too upset that it came true anyway. I was, however, worried about Mom. I wasn't sure what would happen next. I had never had anyone die in my life, so the whole experience was new for me. Family called and checked in on us, but my mom was just a shell of a person. Here she was, a widowed mother of five children (four of them under the age of five). She was the byproduct of a very abusive relationship, but it had been the only real relationship she knew. She had no education and had never worked outside the home. She had been physically and emotionally abused her entire life.

As bad as all of that sounds, my mom had more fear at this stage of her life then she had ever had before or after. Jim's death didn't leave her alone. That would have been much better in her eyes. Jim's death had left her alone to care for five children, with no education, no job, no husband, and worst of all, no hope.

Losing him broke my mom. She tried to take her own life. She saw no way out of the situation she was in.

That fateful day of her suicide attempt was also one of the best days I remember having with my mom. It was as if she was living out the life that she had always dreamed of living. First, she cooked dinner, a type of dinner that rarely crossed our table, even on holidays. She cooked meatloaf, mashed potatoes, and corn. She even baked a cake for dessert.

Then she cleaned the house. It was cleaner than it had been in a long time. She put all of us kids in bed and tucked us in. It was strange for my mom to do this; she had never tucked us in this way before. She kissed our foreheads and told us that she loved us. I hoped this would be the new normal. I prayed that the reason it wasn't like this before was because Jim didn't allow her to be this type of mom. I tried not to fall asleep. I wanted the day to last forever but eventually sleep overtook me.

I awoke to the shrieking screams of the lady who lived next door. She was crying, yelling at my mom to wake up. Then I heard the sirens coming up the street. What was going on? Was the day before just a dream? Was Jim not dead? Had he done this to my mom? It wasn't the first time paramedics had come to our house for Mom. It had to be Jim; who else would have done this to her? I started to cry, not only because I was afraid for my mom but also because I thought Jim was back.

The paramedics worked feverishly to revive her, shocking her over and over again. They desperately blew air into her mouth, trying to wake her up. They shocked her again and then one paramedic said, "I have a pulse!" They strapped her into the gurney and carried her out the door. As the sirens faded down the street, the neighbor lady came up and put her arm around me and told me that everything was going to be okay.

Thankfully, my mom wasn't successful. The medics saved her. She was placed on a psychological hold for patients who experienced mental instability. When she was admitted to the hospital, my siblings and I were split up. I moved in with Gram. My six-month-old sister went to stay with our Aunt Connie, Mom's oldest sister. My three brothers moved in with Jim's sister.

My mom's suicide attempt shook me up. It is heartbreaking for a 12-year-old-boy to learn his mother doesn't want to be alive. I had a lot of emotions running through my mind. But my mom got better. Eventually, she was released from the hospital and able to return home. She decided she was unable to care for all five of us on her own. Instead, she let Aunt Connie adopt my sister, Gloria, and Gram kept me. She did, however, get my three brothers back from Jim's family.

I was going to miss my mom, and my brothers and sister, but I knew it was best I go live with my gram. We had a special bond and I loved her house, even with its chaos of people living there, crashing there, visiting there, and passing through. But when my mom made my gram situation permanent, I was sad. It almost felt like she gave me up too easily. Looking back, I realize it was one of the best things she could have done, and I am so grateful for her strength. But at the time, I felt like a burden who had to be given away.

Gram's house was very stable compared to where I had been so far. There were rules you had to follow and roles you had to fulfill. You had to be in the house at a certain time. You had to take a bath every day. There was always dinner. There were a bunch of other kids who lived within a mile of Gram's house so there was always something fun to do.

There was no Jim. No fistfights. No beatdowns (unless I had to pick my switch for breaking one of Gram's rules) and no getting up at 2:00 a.m. to fix bottles and calm crying babies. I even started to attend school regularly.

Growing up poor, you constantly yearn to have more—more food, more clothes, more furniture, pretty much just more of everything. Being poor, you always feel like you're lacking something. You dream of someday having it all. You dream of a bigger house and lots of cars and toys and clothes and shoes. Very rarely would you think that in some areas of your life you needed less in order to gain. As I look back on my childhood, there were many things that we had far too much of. We had way too much negativity, fear, and doubt. I know I personally had too much hate, anger, and resentment. I even had too much self-pity.

I realize now that those things took up space where all the good things—love, respect, and encouragement—could have been. What you realize is that two things cannot occupy the same space at the same time.

This is true with physical items; it is also true with thoughts and feelings. You cannot hold fear and joy in your mind at the same time. You cannot keep anger and love in your heart at the same time. You cannot have worry and hope in your soul at the same time. In order to have the things that you want or need, you have to get rid of some of the things that you don't need. These things can be physical, or they can be thoughts and feelings. Either way, they need to be removed in order to have the things that you want.

When Jim was killed, it opened up options in my mom's life. She was released from the hospital and working on living a better life. A year after Jim's death, my mom met Pat Burns, her current husband of over 35 years. Pat raised my three brothers as his own sons. Pat was everything that Jim wasn't. He respects and loves my mom and would never dream of hitting her.

My mother is a totally different person today than she was when she was married to Jim. This addition by subtraction is nothing short of a miracle. But it wouldn't have happened if Jim had not left our lives.

I also saw this addition by subtraction in my gram's life once my grandfather was sent away to prison. Gram was stuck in the same situation as my mother. My grandfather was a drunkard and womanizer and never put his family first. He made decent money with the garbage route but never gave much of it to his family. Instead, he chose to drink it away and spend it on others by buying them drinks.

He was also abusive to my grandmother and his kids. I remember hearing stories of my gram and aunts going up to our camp and finding him with women that he had picked up at the bars. She could do little about it and was destined to live the miserable life that awaited her for as long as she was married to my grandfather.

That's not to say she didn't try to do something about it. Family lore has my gram dragging these "bar women" by the hair out of the camp, even one that was nude and passed out next to my grandfather. He never flinched because he was so drunk.

After my grandfather was sent to prison, my grandmother became the matriarch of her family and literally the center of her children's and grandchildren's lives. Everybody respected her and treated her with the reverence she deserved. My gram was loyal and never remarried. She went to visit my grandfather in prison almost every month during his 40 years of incarceration.

But she did not have to deal with him or his habits at home. She was able to raise her family the way she wanted, without alcohol and abuse and fear. She had some of the same fears as my mom did when she lost Jim: how was she going to care for her kids?

Think about your own life. Are there things you now have because you experienced a major subtraction? I bet you can name at least one. It is amazing how we have to lose things to gain the things we really need. It is a lesson I've learned time and time again.

Was it a lesson I was about to learn again as I got closer and closer to losing everything good in my life?

Chapter 14

Into the Deep End

*"Haters will see you walk on water and say it's because
you can't swim"*

— Anonymous

What was I thinking? I didn't know how to run a chain of children's day care centers. I had a business degree, but it was in finance. The only thing that degree would help me with was to see how our finances were going in the wrong direction. There were a hundred different decisions I had to make every day when it came to running these day cares. Where to buy supplies, what supplies to buy, where and when and if we should advertise. What type of insurance should I buy; should I get a warranty on the vans; should I lease the printers or buy them? How big of a price difference should there be between a four-year-old and a six-year-old?

I've never been a details guy. I am a big-picture guy. I just wanted to look at the profit and loss statements and see some black as opposed to all the red that was there now. I was a good commercial real estate agent. I knew how to get deals done, how to negotiate, what made a great site for a tenant, and which sites were losers. Why did I think that just because this Sweet Pea owner was able to run a chain of day cares that I could also do it?

I felt like I was all alone, trying to do something I had no idea how to do. I was sinking and sinking fast, and it brought back a memory.

I was six. My mom and I were at the YMCA, where we could sign up for the free swim. There were very few swimming pools in Bellefonte and none of them belonged to anyone that my family knew. My mom walked me to the pool area and gave me strict orders to stay in the shallow end where I could touch the bottom. She was going to run a few errands.

The pool was your typical small rectangular swimming pool with a diving board on one side and a shallow end on the other. I did what I was told and was wading in the shallow end because I couldn't swim. But then I looked up and saw a kid who looked like he was four or five years old. He was definitely younger than me. I watched him jumping off the diving board and swimming to the ladder. Something clicked in my six-year-old brain that day: if that little kid who could jump off the diving board, then darn it, so could I!

I climbed out of the shallow end and walked to the deep end of the pool to wait my turn in line. No one seemed to doubt that I could do it. No one tried to stop me or even asked if I could swim. I felt very confident.

When it was my turn, I stepped up on the board and looked at the lifeguard, giving him one more chance to talk me out of it. He blankly stared right through me with a look of total disinterest (it was a look I now know is one only a teenaged boy can give).

I went for it. I ran and jumped and then quickly sank to the bottom of the pool. I don't remember panicking when I hit the bottom, I just started walking up the slope that divided the deep end of the pool from the shallow end. After a few seconds I remember my lungs starting to burn and I realized I better go faster so I began to try to run up the slope.

I am not sure if any of you have ever tried to run uphill under water, but it ain't easy. The more my lungs burned, the faster I tried to run and the faster I tried to run, the more my lungs burned. I lost consciousness and had to be rescued and given CPR. The next thing I remember is coughing the water out of my lungs and the same teenage lifeguard staring at me with a much more interested look on his face. I then realized that there were lots of people surrounding me in a circle. Then I remember them all clapping and cheering as I struggled to take a breath. As I looked at all the faces now cheering that I was alive I saw that little kid who had been jumping off the diving board staring at me. I could swear that he rolled his eyes at me, letting me know what an idiot I was.

It was probably just the lack of oxygen to my brain but that's how I remember it.

As the days and weeks went on with me attempting to run these day cares I thought I saw lots of people rolling their eyes at me, and to be honest I was rolling my eyes at myself for ever thinking that I could pull off this miracle of turning these day care centers around.

During those next few weeks, I fell into a dark place in my life. I was depressed, lost, and losing the little hope that I had left. I fell into the "blame game." None of this was my fault, I told myself. I didn't cause the financial crisis, I didn't want to be running day care centers, I didn't cheat my partners, I didn't put us in this position. None of this was my fault. Why was I the one paying the price? Why was it me that had to save these day cares? Where was the justice in all of this? Hadn't I suffered enough? Did I deserve to be suffering for the wrongs of other people? I had been there and done that my entire childhood. Why was I always the one paying the penalties for other people's wrongs? It wasn't fair.

This attitude continued for weeks with my hope and motivation evaporating a little more each day, until one day, when I was making my rounds visiting the day care centers. I was finishing up a call in my car when I noticed a lady getting her kids out of the car and trying to get them into the day care. You could see she was having trouble. There were three young kids. All of them looked like they were under the age of 4. The mother was dressed in scrubs like she worked in a medical office of some sort. She had an infant in her arms as she tried to unbuckle the other two toddlers from their seatbelts. The car was old and beat up. It was clear that it was on its last leg.

She finally got one of the toddlers unbuckled and out of the car. She took him by the hand and walked around to the other back door to get the last child with the infant still in her arms. She opened the door and then pressed the toddler against the beat-up car with her hips so that she had one free hand to maneuver the seatbelt of the last remaining child. The child pinned against the car was not making it easy on his mother. He was wiggling and pushing as hard as he could, trying to escape. After the mother released the seatbelt on the last child, she leaned in to lift him out of the car seat. It was at this time that the child being restrained between his mother's hips and the car made a break for it and ran from his mother across the parking lot just as another car was passing by. The brakes screeched as the passing car attempted to not hit the running child. The mother screamed in horror as she saw the scene play its way out right in front of her.

Fortunately, the toddler was not hit by the car. The mother with one arm holding the baby and the other clinched on the wrist of the other child rushed to the toddler with tears pouring out of her eyes. With her adrenaline peaked, she screamed at the toddler in between sobs. I watched as she herded the three small children into the day care. She came back out still crying and climbed into the beat-up car.

This incident slapped me in the face with a huge reality check. Here was a mother of three doing all she could to provide for them. I later found out that the father of those children had died a year earlier from a drug overdose before the baby was born. This mother was doing all she could with all she had. She had no other options but to do her best.

I felt so small as a person. The fact that I was feeling sorry for myself because I had to figure out how to save a chain of day care centers seemed like nothing. I couldn't believe I had the nerve to feel like I was not getting a fair deal or that I didn't deserve everything that was happening to me.

Was I any less deserving then this sweet mother of three who was trying to provide and raise her children all on her own? You've heard it before: "No matter how bad of a situation you are in, there is someone out there who would kill to be in your situation." It came rushing into my mind, and it had never had as much power as when I watched that old beat-up car pull out of the parking lot.

Chapter 15

The Lifelong Lessons of Uncle Bub

"Courage is knowing what not to fear."

— **Plato**

What if I lose everything? What happens to my wife, my children? What would happen to all the employees who worked at Bright Child and Doggie District? What will people think of me? Is this what people expect? For me, Nelson Tressler, a card-carrying member of the Unlucky Sperm Club, to simply fail after experiencing top-of-the-mountain success? Am I supposed to say, "Screw it," throw my hands into the air and give up?

By now the fear felt real. I could practically smell and taste it. My family depended on me to provide and I was rapidly headed down a path where doing that had become a struggle. With nothing to my name, who was I to the world? Did it even matter?

I needed to dig deep and muster up the courage to carry on. I couldn't worry about the daily "what ifs." They were beginning to consume my every thought: What if the day cares failed? What if the pet resorts go under? What if we lose our home? What if real estate never comes back? What if? What if? What if? There seemed to be too much at stake.

I hadn't felt this kind of fear since I was a child. I wasn't supposed to. I was a grown man now, not a child. But the what ifs came rushing back to crush me just like when I was a child. I just didn't know yet if this time my "what if" was real.

Various cultures have different rites of passage when a person goes from being a child to becoming a man. The Jews celebrate this by having a bat mitzvah, the Catholics celebrate it by having your first communion. But in the small towns of Pennsylvania the rite of passage was when you turned 12 years old: You were able to get a hunting license. Turning 12 was a bigger deal than turning 16 and being able to get your driver's license. (Well, at least for somebody who was under 12 years old it was a bigger deal.)

I vividly remember my first hunting season after I turned 12. My Uncle Bub had a hunting cabin that everybody went up to the night before the season started. As an 11-year-old, you heard awesome stories about what went on at hunting camp. The fact that I was going to be able to go was incredible.

My Uncle Bub would cook a big bowl of chili and bake some cornbread that we would eat over the next couple days while we were at the camp.

(I'm sure there's hunters out there who are reading this who think that chili is about the worst thing you could eat before going into the woods. You know, gas…deer smelling the gas…noise. I think my Uncle Bub thought it was worth it because the gas that chili gave him was worse than anything you'd ever smelled in your life. You would be sitting on one side of the room and all of a sudden, the stench would burn your nostrils. Instinctively, you would clamp your hand over your nose and mouth in a feeble attempt to save your internal organs from dissolving from the smell. Meanwhile, my Uncle Bub would laugh hysterically. It was one of those traditions that no one appreciated except for Uncle Bub.)

There were always nine or 10 people staying at the camp on the first day of buck season. This year was special because three of us turned 12: My cousin Brian, who was Bub's youngest son, my cousin Ralphie, and me. We had talked about this day for months. In fact, we had all gone to the hunter safety course together in July.

You can imagine the mood as we all sat around the fireplace at hunting camp telling stories with the older men. Everybody had dreams of the big buck they were going to get in the morning. Suddenly, the mood shifted as Uncle Bub took on a serious tone.

He told the story of a farmer who had lived on the mountain years ago just up the road from where our camp was. This farmer hated hunters because they would walk through his field and damage his crops. One year he decided to work extra-long a few days before hunting season to harvest and bale his crops so that the hunters would not trample them, rendering them useless. According to Bub, the farmer worked for three days and three nights straight in an effort to bring his crops in before the hunting season opened. It was a full moon the night before opening day, so he was able to work throughout the night.

As he was baling, the hay machine got jammed with a fluorescent orange hunting jacket that a hunter had left in his field. As the farmer tried to cut the jacket loose from his baling equipment, he lost his balance and fell into the baler just as it started to operate again. The man's right hand and his right leg got stuck in the baler all the way up to his kneecap. It made a bloody mess. He was rushed to the hospital where they were able to save his life but not his hand or leg. They replaced his missing hand with a silver hook, and they put a boot on the stump of his leg. His legs were not the same length anymore.

We sat there wide-eyed, listening carefully as Bub continued. Due to the accident, the man was unable to work his land anymore and lost his farm and his home, and was forced to live in the mountains alone. This farmer, who had hated hunters before the accident, now despised hunters and promised to kill any hunter he could get his hands (or, rather, his hook!) on.

Bub said nobody could outrun "Hillside Mooney" if he caught you on the hillside in the woods. In fact, Hillside Mooney had been spotted by one of Bub's friends just up the road from our camp only two nights before. As you can imagine, by this time the three new hunters were almost in tears, although none of us would admit to it. I remember thinking that I would die the next day by the hook of Hillside Mooney. But my Uncle Bub did give us one good piece of advice. He said if Hillside Mooney started to chase you, you were to run in a zigzag motion, and he wouldn't be able to keep up with you. After all, one of his legs was shorter than the other, so he needed to be on uneven ground in order to move as fast as he could.

Just when we thought we had a chance to stay alive, Bub added that Hillside Mooney almost never let anybody see him until it was too late. For good measure, he added that if Hillside Mooney did catch us, he would do what he had done to the hunters that never came home last year. Their remains were never found.

Needless to say, the 12-year-old boys did not get any sleep that night. We stayed up, huddled around the fireplace, afraid to fall asleep. It was one of the scariest nights of my life, but it wasn't half as scary as what I had to go through the next morning.

When you go hunting, you typically go out into the woods before the sun comes up so that you won't spook the deer in the daylight. So as the three 12-year-old boys sat huddled around a fireplace, my Uncle Bub's alarm clock went off and he got up ready for the first day of hunting season. It was still two hours before daylight.

My Uncle Bub gathered me and Brian up in his old International Scout and drove us about a mile and a half down the road where he stopped the Scout and told me to get out. He instructed me to walk down the ridge about 500 yards and find a good spot on the side of the hill where I could see if any deer crossed in front of me. I did not want to get out of the Scout but in my family, you didn't want people to know that you were afraid of anything.

I took a deep breath, grabbed my gun, and forced my legs to move. I climbed out and made my way down the hillside. This was the first time that I had been in the woods alone at night so I was scared anyhow. Add on the story of Hillside Mooney and I was petrified.

There is nothing as quiet as the woods right before dawn. I couldn't hear anything but my heart anyway, banging away like a huge bass drum beating about 1,000 times a minute with all the fear and adrenaline running through me. I slowly made my way down the hill in my fluorescent orange coveralls, knowing that each step could be my last step and that I might soon feel Hillside Mooney's hook in my back or my neck. I swore that every squeak a tree made from the wind blowing was the sound of Hillside Mooney and his hook sneaking up on me.

I am horrified to think of what would've happened if I came across another hunter that morning because I had my gun out in front of me ready to defend myself from the man with a hook. I did eventually make it down to the spot where my Uncle Bub told me to go. The problem was, by the time I made it down there I was scared out of my mind, and too afraid to sit down and wait for daylight in fear that Hillside Mooney would sneak up on me. Instead, I paced back and forth in a zigzag line up and down that hillside looking behind every tree, paying no attention to the noise and commotion that I was making as I did so. I didn't see any deer that morning. Any deer that came near would have had to be deaf, blind, and dumb.

I'm sure most of you would not be afraid to go into the woods after hearing that story as an adult. However, I bet that we are all influenced by other fears that are just as ridiculous in hindsight. Looking back, I am so upset that I was so afraid of something that silly. With a little reasoning and thought, I could've realized that I had nothing to be afraid of and enjoyed the morning.

Thirty-five years later, I have learned an important fact when it comes to fear. It only exists in one place: Your mind. I'm not saying that I am never afraid, I absolutely am afraid at times. But with some coaxing and good self-talk, I can quickly overcome fear when it peeks its ugly head out, or sticks out its hook. Fear is one of those emotions that cripples us and prevents us from taking the steps that are necessary to succeed. I think Franklin D. Roosevelt said it best: "The only thing we have to fear is fear itself."

Fear keeps you tethered in an environment that you know and understand.

Courage is not the absence of fear. It is being afraid and still doing what is needed to be done. We shouldn't be so afraid of death that we never even live. We've all had those moments when we wanted to do something outside of our comfort zone, and then those two crippling words come to our mind, "What if?"

What if things don't go the way I hope they do? What if I fail? What if they don't like me? What if I lose everything? What if, what if, what if, what if. So many opportunities—and unfortunately, dreams—have been lost and not realized after those two crippling words.

Fortunately, my Uncle Bub also gave me a quote that helps me with this "what if" syndrome. I was helping Bub remove catalytic converters from his junk cars at his junkyard. These are the mechanism that attach to the exhaust pipe and prevent pollution from going into the air.

Bub would lift the car with a forklift and then I would go underneath the car and use a hacksaw to cut off the catalytic converter. As he lifted one of the cars with the forklift, the bumper slid off the fork and the car came crashing down as he tried to lift it. Before I saw that car come crashing down, I had already sawed off three or four catalytic converters and had never once thought that the car could actually fall on top of me, but suddenly, I could see it happening. As my Uncle Bub repositioned the forks under the car's bumper and lifted again, he waited for me to crawl under the car to start sawing.

"What if this car falls on top of me?" I asked him.

Bub's response was profound and something that I use to this day, even if it's a bit crude. I think its usefulness outweighs its lack of tact.

"What if your aunt had balls?" he replied.

"What?"

"What if your aunt had balls?"

I repeated what he had just said to make sure I heard him correctly.

"Yeah," he replied. "Then she'd be your uncle. Get under there and saw that thing off."

Bub was not one to over-explain himself, but what I took away from it was that we could literally "what if" ourselves to death. We could ask, "What if," in any situation, no matter how ridiculous. As absurd as the question is, "What if your aunt had balls" is probably not any more absurd than most questions that start with the words "what if?"

I have found a way to use those two words. I just think of them in a different manner. *What if I wasn't feeling this fear? What if I wasn't feeling anxious over this situation? What if I didn't have these doubts? What if I didn't let these feelings stop me?* What if, what if, what if. Those same two words are crippling if used in the wrong way, but they can be liberating if you put a new lens on them.

If we are not careful, fear will be our master. But fear just keeps us confined behind an imaginary fence. It does not exist in reality; it only exists in our minds. Once we learn that and learn to control our minds, we should start asking, "What if we didn't fear?" From there, we will soon realize that it is exactly as Franklin D. Roosevelt said.

In the sweltering heat of Las Vegas as the days dragged on, my mind was full of fear and what ifs. I knew the theory. I knew what I should do. But could I overcome the fear that was not only enveloping me but also the world?

Chapter 16

Blinded by Hunger

"Hungry people are always looking for more. More things to do. More to learn. More responsibility to take on."

— **Patrick Lencioni**

As I walked through the front door at the end of the day, beat up, discouraged, and stressed out, my 11-year-old son, Dawson, came running up to me.

"Dad, can we eat at Geisha House tonight?" he asked eagerly.

Geisha House is a hibachi-style restaurant: The chef puts on a show as they cook the food right in front of you. The kids loved it, especially when the chef made a volcano out of the onion. The rings would overflow with fire and ashes as the chef sprinkled pepper on it. The chef would also pretend to squirt ketchup on you from a trick bottle. It was quite the experience.

The problem was, it was $35 a plate. The way things were going, it would be a long time before we could afford to go to a restaurant that cost $35 a plate, no matter how much my kids loved it.

"Sorry bud, not tonight," I told Dawson gently.

Immediately, he broke into a temper tantrum, crying, throwing himself onto the floor. You would have thought he had not eaten in a week and I denied him a slice of bread. It was a feeling I was familiar with.

Growing up, I was always hungry. And once I got into the commercial real estate business, I was still hungry, but for success. I was perhaps even starving. The ache grew as the financial climate became more and more unsettled. I would come home, stressed to the max. A lot of my stress came from the owners of shopping centers who were stressed because we could not find any tenants. I was hungry for success. They were hungry for profit. The shopping centers were hungry for tenants. But all of us were going without.

The owners of these shopping centers are not really into feelings. They're going to tell you how it is with little tact or empathy. People can treat you horribly, but many times you're willing to deal with it and work with it. There are some developers and owners out there who are going to treat you like dirt without a second thought. You basically eat crap all day, you're never good enough, and you never bring in enough deals.

The whole industry has a lot of thankless components to it. It makes you wonder if perhaps you're better off hungry.

Dawson continued wailing over the fact that he was not going to see the onion volcano tonight. He kept saying that he was hungry and wanted to eat. "Why can't we go, Dad?" he kept asking in between his tears. "I'm hungry, I want to eat. Can we please go, Dad?" The thought that he didn't know real hunger came to my mind as a quick rush of frustration came over me. That thought took me back to a memory from my childhood of me staring at the refrigerator door.

I pulled open the refrigerator door. To be honest, I wasn't really surprised by what I saw. It was more about what I *didn't* see. No matter when I opened the fridge, I'd stare into it, hoping the scene before me would change if I stared long and hard enough. Spoiler alert—it never did. I'd also open the door over and over, hoping that if I opened it enough times, the empty space would be filled with things to eat.

The refrigerator contents were almost always half-used condiments like Miracle Whip, ketchup, mustard, and maybe some relish. You never forget that feeling of emptiness in your stomach and the pain associated with it.

It is, of course, the pain of hunger from lack of food, but it's also the pain of fear, hopelessness, and helplessness. When you combine all these pains together, it is a feeling that you never forget no matter how far away you get from it.

As I said, these experiences are hard, if not impossible, to ever forget. As I sit here, writing this book, I am so far away from that experience, but it is always in the back of my mind. That fear of hunger never truly goes away. In fact, now those fears are multiplied by the fact that there are other people who are depending on me to provide for them.

Those fears are part of what drives me to succeed and to provide for my family so that they never have to experience that pain. As I raised my own family, there were quite a few situations in which my kids thought that they were starving to death because it had been a few hours since they had eaten. My youngest son, Grayson, was notorious for this. He was a fussy eater from the day he was born. He was the kid who couldn't have his corn touch his mashed potatoes. If the two combined somehow, he refused to eat them. The same went for sauces too. *No touchie.* For that matter, he didn't like sauce on anything, not even chicken nuggets, which I think he pretty much lived off of.

Thanks to these fussy eating habits, he sometimes would go long stretches of time without food. When he was younger, he would play and forget that he hadn't eaten and then realize that he was hungry. He would cry and act like he would starve if he didn't eat in the next 30 seconds. And we'd always have to give him whatever he wanted the most. We could never convince him he was far from death.

I often thought how different his eating habits would be if he were in the situation I was in as a child. It concerned me that I was taking away some of the exact situations that have driven me as an adult to succeed and to ensure that my family never went hungry. Had I gone too far? Not only had my family never gone hungry, they didn't even have to eat things they didn't love. Had I taken that hunger away too much?

When you have the *right* hunger in your life, you do the things that you need to do, and there is nobody who can convince you that you are not able to accomplish what you are out to accomplish. You are so blinded by the hunger, just like Grayson, or Dawson, when he was denied the Geisha House, that there is no reasoning, soothing or rationalizing that can pacify you. This type of hunger trumps just about any other talent or skill. You can be the smartest person in the room, the biggest, or the strongest, or the fastest. But without "hunger" you will never take full advantage of those talents.

Hunger also will help you compensate for any lack of talent. In my commercial real estate career, I was always competing against the other top brokers in our market for listings. As I prepared for those listing proposal meetings, I always glanced at the quote on my desk: "If you're not as hungry as I am, don't bother even trying to compete. You're going to lose." Although I didn't win all the assignments, I won many more than I lost. I think the reason for winning most of the assignments was that I remembered that hunger I felt. I wanted to get as far away from it as I possibly could.

One of the greatest gifts of being an Unlucky Sperm Club member is this gift of hunger. There is no other way to give somebody quite the same drive.

There are many different kinds of hungers. As a young child, I went through the literal hunger of not having enough to eat, and I worked hard to make enough money so that I wouldn't have to experience that hunger again or put anyone I loved through it. Then I went through the hunger to improve myself, and I ate up a ton of information from thought leaders so that I could have the knowledge to make better choices. Then came my hunger to succeed, and I have worked as hard as I could to try and reach success in my life. But what I realized, and what this financial crisis was proving to me was that success is not an event, it is a journey that never ends. Success is closely related to true hunger. I live in Las Vegas, the pinnacle of the all-you-can-eat buffet. No matter how much I can eat at one of these buffets, sooner or later I need to eat again. I can't stop eating. Success is the same. No matter how much success you have in your life, if you stop doing the things that have got you to your success, the success will soon go away.

I now have the hunger to inspire and help others. I love how Arnold Schwarzenegger put it: "Be hungry for success, hungry to make your mark, hungry to be seen and to be heard and to have an effect. And as you move up and become successful, make sure also to be hungry for helping others."

I see people living paycheck-to-paycheck to make ends meet. I see people stuck in relationships that don't make them happy and fulfilled. I see people going to work at jobs they absolutely hate. I see people having no purpose in life except to get through another day. But I also have the knowledge that things do not have to be that way. With a few techniques and strategies and lots of action, people can get out of the situations that they are stuck in right now. People who are hungry for a change can make that change. They become hungry enough to wake up every morning. They get to go to a job they love, and they relish their purpose in life. People who are hungry to have fulfilling relationships with significant others. People who are hungry have stability and the resources to not only get by but to prosper.

I have a new hunger. It is to help people achieve and prosper, and live a life that is fulfilling and rewarding. My hunger is to show people that it is possible. Although it's not easy, it is simple. It is painful to see people wandering throughout life with no purpose or direction—and know that that is not the way life has to be. Although they were born into or chose to be in the situation that they are presently in, they don't have to stay in that situation.

I have the hunger to help people help themselves. I have the hunger to help people find the hunger to succeed and to make more out of themselves. I have the hunger to help people be aware of their potential and then to seek possibility after reaching that potential.

I see this potential in everyone. I see the fact that they could have so much more and be so much more and do so much more. It is not the same pain that I felt when I opened that refrigerator door and only saw condiments, but it is similar.

Often we don't see this potential in ourselves, and thus we have no hunger to reach our potential. Sometimes all we need is one person to see that potential and tell us that it's there.

I had several people like that in my life, especially when I was young.

Two of those people were Mary and Chuck Diacont. Chuck was a college student at Penn State University and Mary, his wife, was working as a nurse at the local hospital. I was 11 years old, living with my mom, Jim, and my three younger brothers. It was probably the lowest point of my life. Jim was constantly coming home drunk and beating either my mom or me for no good reason. My mom was often at the bar, leaving us kids with random babysitters or leaving me to watch my siblings. We hardly had any food, and the home environment could not have been worse. But somehow, I got signed up for the Big Brother program. My Big Brother was Chuck.

It was Saturday and I eagerly waited for him to pick me up from Gram's. The normal Saturday routine was underway, with 10 or so adults on the porch surrounding Gram. There were 30 to 40 kids running around. Everybody was excited, knowing my Big Brother was coming to pick me up.

I stood on the porch when a green Toyota Celica turned the corner of the dead-end street. It was the coolest car I had ever seen. To my delight, it pulled into our driveway. A tall, handsome, movie-star-looking guy climbed out. He had a sense of class and dignity about him that was foreign in Coleville. That instant, every single one of my aunts fell in love with him. They all thought he looked like Magnum, P.I. without the mustache. He wore the same type of shorts that Tom Selleck wore. And that Toyota Celica might as well have been a red Ferrari.

"Hey guys, I'm Chuck," he said. I pushed my way through the crowd.

"I'm Nelson," I said.

"Want to grab some ice cream?" he asked.

"Sure."

As I descended the porch steps, I felt like the most important person in the world for the first time in my life. I climbed into his car, feeling so special. I knew the other kids wanted to be me. They wished they were climbing into a Toyota Celica and getting ice cream with a guy like Chuck. We drove into Bellefonte and found a store that sold ice cream by the scoop. The ice cream store was only a half a block down the street from where my pap had shot and killed Officer Seymore. The city of Bellefonte had placed a brass memorial plaque in the sidewalk where Officer Seymore died.

Well, Chuck parked where we would have to walk over that plaque to get to the shop. I broke out in a sweat. As far as I knew Chuck didn't know about my past, and I wanted it to stay that way. I wanted to just be Nelson and not "that Tressler kid." We both got out of the car and started to walk down the sidewalk. I held my breath as Chuck stepped over the plaque and we continued on without any mention of the memorial that represented so much pain in my life.

After getting a cone, Chuck and I walked to Talleyrand Park and sat watching the small waterfall.

"So. Where do you see yourself in 10 years?" Chuck asked me.

I couldn't believe it. Someone actually wanted to know something about me.

And there was more than that. Chuck wanted to hear about what made me happy and what I might want to do in life. He asked me questions that I had never thought of before, like if there were any places I wanted to visit as an adult and what I looked forward to doing.

The questions Chuck was asking were about my future. I answered all of his questions, even though I'd never actually considered that stuff before.

And then Chuck said, in a matter-of-fact manner, "Well, if you're willing to put in the time and the work, you can do everything you told me you want to do, and everything else you put your mind to."

I had never had an adult sit down and have a conversation with me like that before. And no one had ever talked to me about my future.

After about two hours of talking and eating ice cream, he drove me back to my gram's house. By this time, word had gotten out about how good-looking Chuck was. Earlier there were about 10 people on the porch with Gram. Now there were 30, and most of them were my aunts and girl cousins.

When I was with Chuck, I realized for the first time that I could do things if I put my mind to it. Chuck saw the potential in me. I didn't feel like he was looking at me and judging me for who I was. I didn't feel like I was the product of a rape or had the same last name as the trash collector who killed the police officer. I'm pretty sure he knew my circumstances, but he never brought them up and never treated me like I was damaged goods. He treated me like I could do something with my life.

In one of our conversations, Chuck had told me that I would make a good naval officer. He had joined the Navy on the G.I. Bill to get money to go to school. Seven years later, I would do the same thing. Only I would join the Air Force for the G.I. Bill. But the fact that he thought I could be an officer was mind-blowing to me. I was shocked that someone told me I could be something positive. Most of the things that I had heard from adults to that point where how awful I was and how I was going to end up in jail. No one had ever told me that I was someone with potential.

One day, Chuck brought a football with him when we went out for ice cream. I was no stranger to football. I spent half my free time between the telephone poles in front of Gram's playing touch football with my cousins. I could throw and catch. But as we played catch, Chuck continued to compliment me and tell me what a good athlete I was. No adult had ever complimented me the way Chuck did that day.

The next thing I knew, I was signed up for Pop Warner football. To this day, I still don't know how I got registered, but I'm pretty sure it was Chuck who signed me up to play. I excelled at football. They put me on defense and gave me the number 76. I didn't know all the Xs and Os my first year, but the coaches saw that I was not afraid to go after the quarterback and tackle people.

They put me on the end of the defensive line and gave me one command: Tackle the person with the ball. And that's exactly what I did. Chuck and Mary took me to all my games that year. They even brought their friends to watch. Mary took photos with her camera and Chuck and his whole crew would be there cheering me on. I was *somebody* for the first time in my life. I was not in the way. I was not a bother or a burden or a mistake, but I was somebody important. It satisfied a hunger deep within my soul that I never realized I had.

Football showed me I could be good at something, and Chuck and Mary showed me that people believed in me. Chuck eventually graduated from Penn State and moved back to the Philadelphia area where his and Mary's families were from. We still stay in contact to this day and visit each other once a year, typically to go hike some national park together. I don't know where I would be today if Chuck and Mary hadn't come into my life. If I didn't have them to believe in me and to show me that I was important, I may never have realized my worth. They didn't even know me when Chuck signed up for Big Brothers. They just wanted to help and give back.

Their example fuels my hunger to do the same for someone else. The fact that I had such low self-esteem gave me the contrast in my life now to know how truly blessed I am. It helped me realize how important it is to help others around you. Without these experiences, I'm not sure I would have the same urgency or the desire to go and help other people.

I have learned so much since the days I spent longing for a full refrigerator. I learned the secret to a happy life is discovering what feeds you and what you're really hungry for and realizing what you have to do each day to achieve it.

I just had to figure out how to tell Dawson he was getting a peanut butter sandwich instead of Geisha House.

Chapter 17

Becoming a Murderer Myself

"Waste no more time arguing what a good man should be. Be one."

— Marcus Aurelius

When the cracks of the financial crisis started to show in early 2007 so did the cracks of my marriage to Skye. Up until that point, I was so busy with everything I was doing that I hadn't noticed we were growing apart. Before the financial crisis, I was at the top of my game, the perfect provider of the household, nothing like what I knew as a kid. I didn't drink, I didn't hit my wife or kids, I didn't even swear.

I thought I was so perfect, and I got it in my head that Skye was inferior. Each night I would come home from work and expect to have my Stepford Wife meet me in the kitchen with an apron on and three well-manicured young boys sitting around a picturesque dining table. I expected to know there was a pot roast in the oven and a five-course meal prepared for us.

Instead, I'd come home to a messy house, boys with food all over their faces, and a wife who hadn't found time to shower or fix her hair. Skye and I would get into long arguments about how I was the great provider, giving her the lifestyle many women would dream of, and how she was falling short as a mother and a wife. This continued for about a year and a half. Predictably, our marriage deteriorated. The word "divorce" was thrown around. At first, it was uttered on a monthly basis. Then weekly. Eventually, we just stopped talking because every time we did, it was with raised voices and anger.

Then came the fight that was two years in the making. I came home from the office after writing two more checks, one to feed Bright Child, the other to feed Doggie District. My savings were all but gone. As I walked through the door all I could hear was Grayson, my youngest son, screaming at the top of his lungs. When I rounded the corner and looked in the living room, I saw Branson standing over Grayson, apparently having just punched him in the face because Grayson wouldn't share his drink box. Dawson sat on the couch watching cartoons, oblivious to what was going on around him. The house was a mess, with dirty dishes and toys slung all over the place. Where was Skye? She certainly was not in the kitchen cooking. I'm not sure our stove had been used in a month.

I broke up the fight and got Branson his own juice box. I went upstairs to change out of my suit. Skye was in bed, still in her PJs. I wasted no time with the insults and frustrations.

"What in the world are you doing?" I asked. "Didn't you hear what was going on down there? Why are you still in bed? Are you crazy? You're just going to let our kids fend for themselves?"

"I have a migraine," she whimpered, without looking into my fiery, accusing eyes.

"You have something wrong with you every day. Your back hurt last week, your stomach the week before that. Now you have a headache," I retorted.

"I do. I can't even see," she said. Her voice sounded so pitiful that I knew she was faking. No one could be as sick as she was all the time. Her problem wasn't that she was sick. It was that she was lazy, I thought. In hindsight, she could have had blood gushing out of her ears and I still wouldn't have believed her. We were in such a bad place at this time that I only saw what I wanted to see, and at that moment, I wanted to see a wife and a mom who was lazy and had given up.

"I'm done with you. I can't take this anymore. I am leaving. It's over," I said. I put on a pair of jeans and a shirt and grabbed a suitcase. Normally by now Skye would be in the closet with me, pleading for me not to go. She would say she would try and do better. Not this time. I didn't know if I liked the fact that she wasn't begging me to stay or if it scared me that this was really the end. I came out of the closet with my suitcase in hand ready to tell her that there was no talking me out of it this time but she hadn't even moved. She wasn't even crying.

"I'm out of here. I am done with you. Are you not going to say anything?" I asked.

"Just go," she said back, in the most defeated voice I had ever heard. I left not knowing where I was going or what I was going to do. The first night I stayed in a hotel; and then my friend, Aaron (the same guy who would later tell me that my day care manager was on the news), told me I could stay at a house he was using as an office. Skye and I did our best so the boys didn't know what was going on. I came home around bedtime and tucked them in before leaving to go back to my new home. Things were already tough for the kids. I didn't want to make them even tougher.

I had always pictured myself married, living in a big house with the perfect family, a wife who loved and respected me, and I her. But now, it looked like even that would be taken away from me. I loved Skye and I loved our family. How could I have let things get this bad?

It was then I knew I had to destroy someone. This person had no right to live any longer. He was weak. He was headed nowhere fast and the world wouldn't miss him a bit. I don't feel bad about killing this person.

In fact, I think most of us would benefit tremendously by destroying someone. Not just someone but someone who doesn't deserve to exist any longer. Someone not living up to their potential. Someone the world wouldn't miss. Someone their family wouldn't even miss.

Does this sound too harsh to you? You're not alone. Most people will allow these types of people to exist as long as they can. They will let them exist in their unfulfilling lives. But why feel bad about getting rid of someone like that? Why feel bad for someone who's just taking up space and bringing most of the people around them down?

I'm talking about the father who sucks at being a father. He won't provide the lifestyle or leadership his family deserves. He never goes out of his way to talk to or teach his kids. He is out of shape and unhealthy and has no energy to do the things he knows he can and should do. Get rid of him!

Or the mom who would rather play Candy Crush all day and order takeout for her family instead of cooking a meal with her kids and making good memories. I say eliminate her! What about the 20-something who is just coasting through life, putting forth as little effort as they can? They are just surviving, going to a job they hate that is not fulfilling, just to get a paycheck. Get rid of them and do it quickly.

I'm talking about getting rid of *ourselves*.

Not suicide, of course. That is never the answer. I am talking about getting rid of that version of yourself that is well below where you can and should be living your life. I had to get rid of the unfair, selfish Nelson. I had to eliminate the Nelson who got mad at his beautiful wife for not living up to the unachievable expectations and fantasies he had built.

I had to readjust my ideals of what a family should look like, and instead embrace what my family actually was. I had to eradicate my own prejudices and start fresh.

I knew I had to wipe out the bad father and husband living in me and keep on trying with Skye. But I didn't know how to do that just yet.

We all have two lives: The one we are living and the one we are capable of living. The way we form these new lives is by making better choices. These better choices make better people. Our potential to be great is limitless but so is our potential to be bad. I needed to start making some better choices in a lot of the areas of my life and I needed to start now, before it was too late.

Chapter 18

Dog-Gone-It

"Give the world the best you have, and the best will come back to you."

— Madeline Bridges

When things are so wrong for so long, you take solace in small things that you would have barely noticed in better times. The few months since discovering my Sweet Pea day care centers were being run by am embezzler had not been great—but strangely, they weren't horrible either. I'm not sure whether I got used to the uncertainty that was going on around me or if things were indeed starting to get better.

I did realize that I was trying to be more positive. I was trying to focus on what I could do and not what was happening in the world as a whole. I was focusing on changing the way I treated my wife and children, not how they were treating me. I was focusing on what I could do to help turn the day cares around and not what my ex-partner had done to me and my father-in-law. And best of all was that I didn't have to think or do much with Doggie District. Austin was doing well and needed less and less guidance in the operations. Doggie District was the one shining thing in my life until the call came in.

"I have to tell you something," Austin said, sobbing into the phone.

"Ok, calm down Austin, what's going on?" I replied.

"It's bad," he said. "I'm so sorry."

"Start from the beginning."

"The yard attendant was taking out the trash and left the gate open," Austin said.

Okay, a dog must have gotten out. We could find a lost dog.

"One of the dogs in the yard bolted out the gate."

This was going how I predicted.

"He ran into the street and got hit by a car," Austin said with a gasp.

Oh no.

"He...didn't make it."

Oh no!

Beads of sweat started to form on my brow as my face grew flush. We had dogs get hurt or get in fights before, but this was total neglect. We were done for. There wasn't a thing we would be able to do.

"Did you notify the owners?"

"Not yet, I wanted to call you first to determine what is next," Austin replied.

"We're going to have to call them. Do you think you can do that?" I asked sarcastically, with lots of irritation in my voice. This was the end for Doggie District.

There was a pause as Austin tried to process what he'd have to do. "Yeah."

"You might want to start packing up your desk. This is the end," I said sharply.

"Yeah," was all he could say.

I was furious. At this point, every time I got a call or an e-mail it was more bad news. I was at wits' end with the bad luck. I had invested hundreds of thousands of dollars on this dog day care. I had fed it with cash for years in hopes that we would make it out of this crisis, but this had to be the last nail in the coffin. We were done. There was no coming back from this. What a waste.

Austin called me back, still in tears, after he had delivered the horrible news.

"Well, did they call the news and tell them we killed their dog?" I snarled.

"I don't know, Nelson, they weren't happy," Austin said.

"Duh, no kidding. We killed their dog," I retorted.

Austin started to cry again on the other end of the phone. "They have another dog here that they are coming to pick up tomorrow morning. They said we could talk more then. They needed to digest everything that had happened."

"Well, try not to let that dog die before they get there," I said, and hung up the phone. I was *still* furious. We were trying so hard to hang on to everything and now this.

But even by then I already understood it wasn't Austin's fault. He was the reason that we were still open and had a chance of getting out of this fiasco, but I had no one else to blame at the time. And this incident had instantly put me in a blame state of mind.

That night I didn't sleep a wink. I knew the next day would be the end of Doggie District. We would lose everything.

I stopped by Doggie District on the way into the office. Austin was there with bloodshot eyes and huge weary bags beneath them. He hadn't slept at all. If I didn't know better, I would have thought that he stayed at the resort holding the client's other dog all night, ensuring that nothing happened to that one.

I had planned to tell Austin how he had let us all down, and how this was going to be the end for not only us but for every employee that worked at Doggie District. But I couldn't do it. I saw the pain in those tearful eyes. Austin was more hurt for the clients who had lost their dog then he was concerned for what would happen to the business. He was *concerned* for the business but losing someone's dog totally destroyed him. Seeing him in that condition, knowing that he was thinking more about the clients then what happened to him, instantly softened my hard, callous heart. His heart was in the right place. He wasn't thinking about himself and his needs. He was thinking about two people who had just lost a member of their family; how bad it was hurting and how deep their loss was.

That day, I became the consoler instead of the condemner. I told him that no matter what happened, it wasn't his fault. That we would figure it out and get through it.

"I feel so bad for the owners. They lost their dog because of me," was all he said to me.

I left and went to work expecting the worst and praying for a miracle, although I didn't know what the miracle could be.

Austin filled me in later. He said that the clients came to pick up their other dog and they brought something with them. The wife had baked Austin and the staff cookies. You read that right: *Cookies.* As distraught as the clients were over the death of their dog, they knew that Austin and the staff of Doggie District were just as heartbroken as they were. They didn't blame Austin. They knew how much he loved the dogs that came there. They attributed it to the horrible accident that it was and forgave all involved.

These clients had been coming to Doggie District for years. They told Austin that they knew how much he loved these dogs and that he would never allow anything to purposefully happen to them.

Austin told me they hugged and cried together and then the clients took their remaining dog and left. That is, until they showed up three days later with—you guessed it—another plate of cookies and their remaining dog, to be dropped off for day care.

It was the miracle I had prayed for. I hoped it wasn't the last.

Chapter 19

The #48

"Your family is the best team you will ever be on."

— Anonymous

Skye and I were still deciding if we wanted to be married. We'd inflicted a lot of pain on each other over the last few years. Seeing how tired Skye was of fighting me the night I left, and then witnessing the way our Doggie District clients had handled the death of their dog, had put me in a new frame of mind: I was trying to be a better person, trying to let go of all the expectations of what I thought I wanted. I was trying to replace those expectations with appreciation for what I had. I was still living in Aaron's office and had been for a few months, but I still came home every night to tuck in the boys. We were working hard to keep the truth from them, hanging on to a shred of hope that our marriage would survive, and it worked. Their youth and my already-busy business schedule helped: they had no clue I wasn't living at home.

Dawson and Branson played Little League baseball at the time, and I met up with my family at all their games. We put on our happy faces so the boys and no one else knew we were separated. Watching the boys play baseball. Taking pride in how they did. These were common things Skye and I shared. We wanted the same things. We wanted our boys to be happy and productive. We wanted a happy family. I still loved her, and she still loved me. If we could just get past all the hurt and mistakes of the past few years, maybe we could start over and somehow some way make it work.

We sat next to each other in the stands watching our son's baseball game, hoping no one noticed the distance between us when eight-year-old Branson came up to bat. He wore the number 48, the same number I'd worn in junior high football and in my college football days. Skye's dad had worn the same number when he was in high school sports. Branson stood at the plate and waited for the pitch. He was on a hitting streak and had recently hit a few balls to the fence. One hit the centerfield fence on the fly but he had not hit one over the fence yet.

The first pitch was a ball, high and outside. Branson repositioned himself in the batter's box and prepared for the next pitch. It was right down the middle and Branson swung with all his might. The ball was lifted high in the air and made its way towards the left field fence. The left fielder started to backpedal as the ball went over his head. The ball kept going and going and going. Home run! Over the fence! Skye and I jumped out of our seats, into each other's arms, and kissed before we knew what was happening.

Branson trotted around the bases with his arms out to his side as he crossed each base. Skye and I were ecstatic for the first time in a long time as we watched number 48 cross home plate with his arms outstretched like wings and a big smile on his face.

Celebrating Branson's big win together was the moment we both realized we wanted to try again to make this marriage work and try to save our family. We had a lot of work ahead of us. We both knew that it was going to be a long road back. But seeing that number 48 crossing the plate brought back memories of how hard I could work when I really wanted something.

It was the first day of tryouts for my junior high football team. I was extra excited this year. It would be the first time I was playing for the school football team. I had played the previous three seasons in a recreational league and had some good success. I had started both offense and defense as a linebacker and running back. But this year was different. This year I wanted to try out for quarterback.

The quarterback position had never really interested me in the recreational leagues. All the quarterback did was hand the ball off to the running backs 40 times a game. Our team rarely ever threw the ball at that level. However, at the junior high level, they actually threw the ball a few times a game. Better yet, they ran the option, which is when the quarterback reads the defense and decides who gets the ball based on what the defense presents. Many times, that leads the quarterback to keep the ball to himself and run it.

At the junior-high level, the quarterback was the main focus of the offense, unlike in the recreational league, where the running backs were the focus. I had worked hard all summer. I had spent the season working on the back of a garbage truck, lifting a thousand garbage cans and bags a day. After work every day I lifted weights and ran several miles to make sure I'd be at the top of my game when tryouts began.

Almost every night that summer we played football in between the telephone poles on Gram's street. I was, of course, the quarterback and threw hundreds of passes a day to my cousins and friends. By the end of the summer, I could throw the ball 50 yards in the air and hit the receiver even if he was at a full sprint.

The morning of tryouts, I woke up like a kid on Christmas. After warm-up and stretches, the coaches told the players to go to the offensive position that they wanted to play. The kids who wanted to be lineman would go one place, the running backs would go to another, the receivers to another—and the quarterbacks would stay with the head coach.

I stayed with the head coach. I was nervous but also confident. I had put a lot of work and effort into this. There were four players, including me. I knew the other three. There was the kid who played quarterback for the recreational league that I was on. There was another kid whom I knew from school—I hadn't known he played football. And then there was the backup quarterback from last year's junior high team. He was a year ahead of me in school.

The coach had us get 10 yards from each other and throw the ball back and forth to warm up. I quickly positioned myself across from the kid who was the backup quarterback on last year's junior high team. His name was Brandon McMurtry. We started out throwing nice, easy passes back and forth to each other. After about 10 throws each, the velocity picked up on our throws. His throws would come to me a little bit harder and I was obliged to send it back just a little bit harder than his throw.

Brandon must've picked up on this because he sent the ball back to me just a little harder than I had sent it to him. By the time the coach told us to circle around him, Brandon and I were throwing 80 mph fastballs at each other, trying not to flinch or show how much it hurt our hands catching the balls.

The coach with the receivers joined us and we lined up to throw them 10-yard passes.

This was a pass I had practiced all summer between the telephone poles. "Set, hut!" I said, and took my three-step drop. I planted my back foot and waited for the receiver to make his turn. Just as the receiver made his turn, I threw the ball and it went exactly where I aimed, hitting him in the chest. I threw seven or eight more curls in this drill with the same results and accuracy. So far, so good.

We then moved on to throwing post patterns: The receiver sprints down 10 or 12 yards and makes a cut towards the goalpost. We had practiced this at Gram's too. Finally, the receivers ran a go pattern. That just meant that they tried to outrun the person covering them. This was the most popular pattern between the telephone poles. We always wanted to score and score quickly, and this was the play that would do it, if the receiver could get behind the defender and the quarterback could throw the pass accurately.

I decided this would be the drill where I'd show my arm strength. On a go pattern, the quarterback determined when he threw the ball and how far he let the receiver run down the field before he threw it. My first few throws, I hit the receiver at about 30 yards. The two other quarterbacks hit the receiver at about 20 yards. Brandon, not to be outdone by me, was also hitting the receivers at about 30 yards.

I then let the receiver run to about 40 yards before I threw the ball. Brandon did the same. Then I let them go to 50 yards and threw the ball with all I had, letting him run under the pass in full stride and catch the ball. With the catch complete, I stole a glance at the coaches. The head coach and the receiver coach talked to one another as they watched. The receiver coach had a big smile on his face and was laughing as the receiver caught my 50-yard bomb. But the head coach looked serious and unimpressed.

Brandon was up next. Of course, he tried to let the receiver run to 50 yards before he threw the ball. He came up short. It was my turn again, and I was determined to show that my first 50-yard pass was not a fluke. I let the receiver go 50 yards again and again and again. I hit him every time. Once again, I glanced over at the coaches. The receiver's coach was giddy. The head coach was still not. After the throwing drills, it was crystal clear I had the best arm out of the four quarterback options.

Next was the read option drills with the running backs. The coaches showed us every option and tested to see if we could pick up which one was going on in the defense. They wanted to see if we were making the right decisions. I loved running this option. I was able to pick up exactly what the defense was doing and make the right calls. For the most part, the other quarterbacks could do the same thing. Brandon definitely knew what he was doing. He had played in this offense last year and had plenty of practice.

After the option drills the coach called us all together. We were going to run the 40-yard dash. I couldn't wait. I'd always been one of the fastest kids on the team. We made two lines and the coaches lined up with whistles and stopwatches. You raced the person that came up in the opposite line from you. I made sure to count off the numbers so that I would come up against Brandon. That was exactly what happened. We came up to the line, looked at one another, and waited for the whistle.

As the whistle sounded, we both took off. It was clear from the start that I was a lot faster than Brandon. I beat him by a full second, which is a lot over a 40-yard dash. I was sweating with confidence.

Practice ended and we circled up. The coaches told us to return at the same time the next morning. I went home elated: It was a no-brainer. I was destined to be quarterback.

The next day, I returned to the field and we broke off into offensive positions. This time there were only three quarterbacks. The kid who'd been quarterback for the recreational league had decided to go with the tight ends.

The second practice was very similar to the first practice and again I felt like I outthrew and outran the other contenders. We threw some different patterns, and for the most part my accuracy was spot-on. At the end the practice, instead of running the 40-yard dash, we ran the cone drill. This consisted of sprinting to one cone and then backpedaling to the next cone; sidestepping to the next cone and then sprinting through the last cone. This was done individually, and the coaches used the stopwatch to record your time.

I had the best time on the team. Not just the quarterbacks, the *whole team*. All the work that I put in that summer was paying off and there was little doubt that I would win the starting job.

The next day, we received our shoulder pads, helmets, and pants. After getting fitted for the pads and helmets, the coaches told us to go to the defensive positions we wanted to try out for. Even though I had been a linebacker in the recreational league, I had no interest in playing that position at this level. I was all of 5 feet, 8 inches tall and 140 pounds soaking wet.

I tried out for the cornerback position. The cornerback's main responsibility is to defend the pass. And if anybody would happen to get past the defensive line, cornerbacks would be the last line of defense to tackle them. I thought I had a pretty good chance of starting at this position because of my speed and the fact that I was not afraid to come up and smack somebody. I went with the cornerbacks and safeties when we split off for the defense drills.

Those drills went well, and my speed really showed compared to the other kids trying out for that position. At the end of that practice the coach called us all in and we made two lines between the bags. When it was your turn, you went up to the bags and laid on your back across from the player in the opposite line. He would lay on his back as well about 10 yards away. The coach would blow the whistle and then both players would bounce up, turn around, and hit the player from the opposite line.

I loved to hit, and I loved this drill. When it was my turn, I looked across to see what player I would be going up against. I was so excited to see it was a player about my size. I laid down, clenched my fist, and waited for the whistle to blow. The sound pierced the air. I sprung up, swung around, and sprinted with all of my might towards the player at the opposite end of the circle. I hit him with everything in me, square in the chest. He dropped like a sack of potatoes. The rest of the team erupted in cheers.

I quickly turned to look at the coaches, hoping to catch their reactions. I could tell they were impressed. The next time up, I came up against a big kid from the offensive line. TJ Perryman was the biggest kid on the team, weighing close to 300 pounds. I lay there with my fist squeezed in white-knuckle fashion, ready to spring and hit this much larger kid with all I had. The whistle sounded, and I was up and at a full sprint before Perryman could even get out of his stance. In seconds I was on him, hitting him with full force before he took a step. He didn't fall like the smaller kid but I rocked him back. Once again, the guys cheered.

My confidence was going through the roof now. I'm a little embarrassed to say that by this time I was getting cocky. Instead of leaving my opponent up to chance, I looked to see where Todd Hardy was. He had also destroyed both of his opponents and the team had cheered his accomplishments as well. I wanted to show that I was not afraid of somebody who was 50 pounds heavier than me and five inches taller. So I counted the players and put myself in line opposite of Todd. When it was our turn, the guys let out an "Ooooo."

I laid on my back. At the first tweet of that whistle I sprung up as fast as I could. I could see that Todd had sprung up just as quickly. We ran toward each other at full steam and met in the middle with a thunderous crack.

I didn't knock Todd on his butt, but he didn't knock me on mine either. After the hit, we both just stood there looking at each other. Neither one of us wanted to concede defeat. It was a stalemate. However, it was a win for me. Todd should have put me on my butt but he didn't. Todd's friends who were smacking him on the butt just seconds before were now scowling at me. I quickly glanced over at the coaches again and saw respect in all their eyes, including—finally!—the head coach's.

The next day, we received our game uniforms, including our jerseys. The jerseys were laid out on three or four card tables in order from lowest to highest number. In football you get a number based on what offensive or defensive position you play. Lineman get numbers in the middle, from 50 to 79. Receivers get numbers in the 80s, running backs numbers from 20 to 49. Quarterbacks are assigned numbers from 1 to 19. The three of us who were trying out for quarterback got first choice of what number we wanted.

Brandon had played the previous year, so he automatically got his number: Seven. It was then my turn to pick. We lived close to Penn State University, and they'd won the national title a few years before with Todd Blackledge, so I quickly snatched up number 14. Then the rest of the team went in and picked their jersey numbers. I thought I was going to do Todd Blackledge proud when I won the starting position. I also took note that my number was twice as big as Brandon's number, and in my mind, I figured I was at least twice as good as him, so it made sense.

But at the end of practices, the head coach and assistant coach called me into their office. I thought for sure they were going to award the starting quarterback position to me and tell me how proud they were. Instead, it was the opposite. They started out by complimenting me on my toughness and my speed. Then they said that they had a great idea on where I could play. There was no one that was a standout at defensive end. And from what they had seen me doing in the drills, particularly not being afraid to go up against the biggest kids on the team, they thought the defensive end would be the best position for me to play.

"Nelson, we can't have a quarterback play that position," they said. They came up with four or five reasons why a quarterback couldn't play defensive end. I don't even remember what they were. My head was swimming.

"I understand, but I'm here to play quarterback. That's the position I came to try out for. I'm okay if that means I can't play defense," I said.

"Nelson, that is not what is best for the team."

"But I'm so much better than Brandon! Did you see me in the drills? I threw further and with more accuracy than the other guys. I'm faster at the 40-yard dash. I spent the entire summer preparing for these tryouts."

My pleas fell on deaf ears. The harder I tried to convince them, the more irritated they became. I realized I was fighting a losing battle. They told me that they wanted me to move to running back on offense and play defensive end on defense. I left the office depressed and frustrated. I sat down at my locker as tears started forming in my eyes.

"What's going on?" my friend Matt asked.

"They want me to play defensive end. I can't be quarterback." I explained.

What he said next totally floored me. "Dude, you never had a chance at starting quarterback."

"What are you talking about? I'm 10 times better than Brandon!"

"Doesn't matter how much better you are. The only thing that matters in Bellefonte when it comes to playing quarterback is who your daddy is."

"Matt, what are you talking about?"

"If your daddy ain't nobody, you're not starting quarterback in Bellefonte. Think about it, Nelson. Look at who the quarterback was last year. Do you know who the announcer for the varsity game is?"

"Yeah, his dad." I said.

Matt nodded. "And the varsity team starting quarterback this year is Doug Sieg, from one of the richest families in Bellefonte."

"Yeah but he was worthy of the position and going to a Division I school when he graduated. Probably even to Penn State," I retorted.

Matt quickly shot back, "Not always the case."

Matt knew Bellefonte football history a lot better than I did. His two older brothers had played, and he had heard stories of people who tried out for quarterback and been passed over because their dad wasn't a prominent figure. Matt was my best friend, and even he couldn't overlook the fact that there was no way a Tressler was ever going to be a starting quarterback.

"Dude," he said, "you're the last person that's ever going to be a quarterback in Bellefonte."

It couldn't be true, could it? It wasn't a real thing. There was no way that coaches cared who your dad was.

I didn't sleep much that night. There were so many things running through my head. I was no stranger to being left out because of where I came from. But I never thought that those prejudices would follow me onto the football field. That was why I loved football. You could prove who you were by what you did on the field. It didn't matter what your last name was. The better player was the better player. At least, that's the way it had been in the recreational leagues. But maybe Matt was right. Maybe I didn't stand a chance because of who I was. I couldn't get that thought out of my head all night.

The next day at practice after warm-ups, it was time to split up to our offensive positions. I just stood there for what seemed like an hour when everybody else went to where they were supposed to be. With regret that I still feel to this day, I turned and ran towards the running backs. After that practice, the head coach called me into his office again and complimented me on how proud he was that I was willing to do what was best for the team. He could tell I was upset, but he said in the long run this would be what was best for me and the team.

I just shook my head, knowing that I had had no choice in the matter. Then I got up to walk out of his office.

"Take that number 14 and turn it in for a running back number," he told me. It was his way of telling me not to think twice about the decision I just made. It was final. No takebacks. I went to my locker and took out the number 14 and walked to the equipment room where the leftover jerseys were. It was slim pickings by now. The other 65 or so kids on the team had already picked their jersey numbers and there were not very many left. One stood out. The number 48 sat there, half balled-up on the table.

That's how old my grandfather had been when he shot the police officer.

There was no doubt why I was in that equipment room turning in the number 14 for a different number. I picked up the number 48 and held it up. This would be what would drive me to succeed in sports—not only on the football field but in every sport I played. Every time I put on the number 48, it would remind me that life is not fair. That people don't always do the right thing. But I was not going to let this destroy me.

Every time I put on the number 48, I would prove to the world that I was not just going to roll over and die. I was going to put forth every ounce of energy and effort to prove to people that I could succeed, and that there was no denying that number 48 was the best player on the field no matter what position he played.

Brandon was named the starting quarterback that year. I ended up starting at defensive end and racked up 10 or 15 sacks and more than 30 tackles behind the line of scrimmage. I was named "Hustle Captain" six of our eight games. This was given to the player who had had the best game. Every time I went on the field, I wanted to show those coaches that I was the best player there. That didn't stop at junior high. It continued all the way through high school where I started both offensive and defensive my junior and senior years and was named first-team All-Conference.

There are so many times in our lives when we feel like we are not getting a fair shake. We have two choices: we can let what we perceive to be unfair destroy us or we can let it fuel us.

One of my favorite quotes of all time is from Tony Robbins: "Things only have the meaning you're willing to give them." This is so powerful. We get to assign meaning to everything that happens to us in this life. We are the authors. We can give just about anything that happens to us a negative meaning or just about anything that happens to us a positive meaning. We get to choose. And if we get to choose, why on earth would we ever choose to give something a bad meaning? Life is not fair—but another quote that I like better is that if life were fair, horses would get to ride you half the time. So thank goodness life's not fair. Thank goodness we get to assign the meaning we want to every situation that happens to us.

I now needed some of that drive to help me do my best in life. I needed to get through the seemingly unfair things that were happening to me now. I needed to stop blaming and look for ways I could regain control. Could the number 48 motivate me to get through what I was going through? I think it could, only I wasn't wearing 48 anymore. My boys were, and because of that I was even more motivated to succeed.

Chapter 20

Just Move the Chains

"You only need to take a series of tiny steps, consistently, over time, to radically improve your life."

— Darren Hardy

My father-in-law and I owned and operated six Bright Child Learning Centers. Owning was one thing, operating was a completely different animal. It was an expensive venture. It cost nearly $10,000 a center just to change the logo and put up a new sign. Then we had to change everything associated with the brand, including paperwork, name tags, and advertising.

I had zero experience with operations. When I opened Doggie District, I gave Austin the reins. I was a dealmaker, not a business operator. And with children on the line, there are all sorts of licenses, inspections, hiring practices, and safety procedures that need to be followed. Standards have to be met, paperwork has to prove the standards were met, staff needs to stay up on their training, and more.

The cherry on top of this very expensive cake was that none of the day cares brought in positive cash flow. Everything was in the red, and that red was in the process of turning blood red. I had to figure out how to make the centers reputable and profitable, quickly. The name change was the easy part, but the day cares had a culture that was poison. You know the saying: You can dress a pig up and make it wear lipstick but it is still a pig. Yeah, in this case, that "pig" was Sweet Pea's reputation, both internally and externally.

The previous owner had lied and cheated, and he had also abused the staff for as long as any of them were willing to take it. Most of the staff didn't have any better alternatives because of the economy. They were stuck. Years of mistreatment had left many of the staff jaded and disgruntled. Nearly all were almost impossible to motivate and train. They didn't trust me or believe me when I told them I was going to do something different. I couldn't get them to go all-in on things that would hopefully make the centers profitable. I'd hold meetings and carefully go over the way things needed to be done. The staff would listen, nod their heads yes, and when I left the premises, they would go back to doing things the way they had always done them. Habits die hard and attitudes are difficult to change. It wasn't just one center; it was all of them. I thought to myself, I just need to fire everyone and start over. Trade all these employees in for new ones.

I needed something big to happen. Something to snap them out of their know-it-all ways and see that I was serious.

There have been many times in my life where the solution felt so clear-cut that I couldn't understand why others were hesitant to adopt my way of thinking. I wanted to scream, "This is going to be better for all of us." But they didn't believe me. They were going to do what they were going to do. And they might lose their jobs because of it.

I was torn: Should I make a big bold statement and fire a lot of the staff to get their attention? They'd know I was serious then. Or should I take the long-term approach and earn their trust as we continued to work together?

Earning trust hadn't failed me yet. On my high-school football team, we loved drawing up trick plays that, when executed correctly, were sure to score a touchdown. We came up with a play that had a double-reverse pass back to the quarterback. I was left-handed, so the second reverse was me going to the left where the quarterback had run to the end zone after making the *first hando*ff. In our teenage minds, this was a can't-miss play. We had proved as much when the coach let us run it in practice.

Flash-forward to the Friday night game. It was late in the fourth quarter and we were down by two. It was a home game, so the fans were going crazy. If you have ever been to a small-town football game on a Friday night, you know exactly what I'm talking about. They shut down the town for the football games. And this year we were so good, even the fair-weather fans were out to cheer us on.

We were on the 35-yard line going in. It was second down and two yards to go to get a first down. The other team called a time-out to come up with a plan to stop us on this important play. Perfect timing. This pause would give us a chance to call the double-reverse pass. I was smiling ear-to-ear when the coach came out from the sideline. The first thing I did when he got there was yell, "Let's run the double reverse pass. It's perfect timing."

The coach looked at me and shook his head. "No, we have plenty of time on the clock. We just need to move the chains."

"But coach, if we miss it, we still have two downs to get the first down."

My protest prompted additional protests from the huddle.

"Guys, we just need to move the chains and get in position for a field goal," coach said. We had a great field goal kicker who was almost automatic from about 30 yards out. We were only seven or eight yards away from him being able to win it for us.

"Coach, come on, we can win it on this play. They will never expect us to run a play like this in this situation," I said. We had three plays to get two yards. I don't think any of us doubted we could do that. I don't think this team had stopped us in the back field all night. It was too easy.

I rallied. "Coach, if we don't get a touchdown on the double reverse, we promise to get the two yards on the next down, right guys?"

The guys cheered and chanted, "Yes! Yes! Yes!" Coach knew he had lost this one.

"Ok, it's your team. Run it." he said.

The quarterback called the play. "Fifty-two double-reverse pass on one. Break!"

We broke the huddle, our faces beaming under our helmets as we swaggered to the line of scrimmage. The quarterback started the cadence "Blue twenty-one! Blue twenty-one! Set hut!" The ball snapped and the quarterback handed the ball off to the tight end as the quarterback took off for the end zone. The tight end ran parallel to the line of scrimmage and handed the ball off to me. The other team didn't have a clue what was going on. They were going left, then running right. I even saw one of the linebackers just stop and watch, he was so confused.

I ran with the ball to the left. There was no one on the left side. I could have run for 20 yards until someone touched me. Then I looked up and saw the quarterback in the end zone waiting for my touchdown pass. I could almost hear the talk tomorrow in all the shops around town about how I'd thrown the game-winning touchdown pass. I set my shoulders, cocked my arm back, and threw the pass. As soon as it hurled into the air, I knew it was right on target. Then my heart stopped in my chest. I thought we had fooled everyone on the opposing team. But one of the guys had caught on. The safety had not bit on the first reverse *or* the second. He'd stayed back and made sure no one got behind him, including the quarterback coming out of the backfield. Seconds later, he jumped in front of the quarterback and intercepted the ball. I was sick. I had cost the team the season so I could be the hero in spectacular fashion.

Without warning, our quarterback exploded on the safety and the ball came loose. I was so relieved, I jumped and screamed out loud. Coach called a time-out.

"You boys got that out of your system? Ready for me to call the game again?" he asked. "Let's move the chains!

We ended up scoring a touchdown on that drive, winning the game. We eventually went on to win the championship that season.

I learned a valuable lesson that day. It's not about being sexy and doing things with lots of flair. Sure, we all enjoy it when that happens. We enjoy watching it happen, but the surefire way to success is to just move the chains.

Darren Hardy wrote one of the best books I've read on this concept, *The Compound Effect*. He uses lots of examples in which small, consistent actions reap awesome results. And through these small choices you can trade the life you have for the life you want.

My youngest son, Grayson, could teach me about good trades.

My sons are big baseball players. They have been playing since they were five or six years old. They play Little League and club ball, which has traveling teams. One of the traditions with these traveling teams is to get a pin specifically designed for your team. It is also common that these travel teams split up on a regular basis. This happens for a variety of reasons, often due to coaches moving on, people moving away, or parents getting disgruntled because their kid doesn't bat first in the lineup, play shortstop, or get his favorite jersey number.

It is quite dramatic. I think someone could make a reality show centered around club baseball.

That being said, we've had the opportunity to be on lots of different teams and thus collect lots of different pins. These pins were like badges to the kids on each team. Hours upon hours are put into the design of these pins and every team tries to outdo one another to have the coolest pin out there. Some teams have hired graphic designers and spent thousands of dollars on the designs of their pins. And there *are* some pretty awesome pins out there. But what the players love to do is trade pins before and after the games.

Then some genius came up with the idea to design pins that are not associated with any team but are very cool. These pins range from gorillas to dragons to flame heads to scorpions. I'm not sure what type of value system the boys have on these pins, or how they come up with those values, but they know what's a good trade and what is a bad trade and how many gorilla pins are worth a flame-head pin or how many spider pins you should get for a gorilla pin.

Grayson is a master pin-trader. He knows exactly what he wants, and he knew exactly what he was willing to give up to get a certain pin. He would come home and show us what he traded for certain pins and laugh because of what a good deal he felt he got.

One time, he felt bad that he had traded three "garbage" pins, as he called them, for one "dinner plate." Dinner plates are big nice pins that you typically have to buy; they're a rare trade. They are in the shape of some really cool animals or character that all the kids want. One day, he had traded three pins that were worthless to him to get one of these big dinner plates. That night, he started to feel bad about it, and we talked about what happened. He told me that the boy that he was trading with really didn't know what was going on and what the value of these pins were. Grayson said that the pins that he traded were worthless and that he got this great pin that there were only a few of. He felt a little bad because it was such a bad trade for the other boy.

"How much is this great pin worth if you bought it from someone with cash?" I asked him.

"I don't know. But I've had to trade nine pins to get a pin like this before," he said.

"Do you feel like you were dishonest in your trade?"

"No, I offered him three pins and he took it."

"Was the boy happy with the three pins you traded for the bigger pin?"

"Yes, he was happy with the trade. He seemed like he really liked the pins I traded him."

"Then why do you think it wasn't a good trade? The boy was happy."

Grayson is a very analytical thinker. He is very intelligent, so he was working this scenario through in his mind in only a way that I wish I could. He was making sure that he understood exactly all the angles and options of what I just told him.

"So if I am happy and he is happy, it was a good trade," Grayson said.

"Exactly. That's the way every deal should work. They should all be win-win situations. Do you feel like you won this trade?"

"I do!"

"Do you think the other boy feels like he won this trade?"

"I guess he wouldn't have traded me if he didn't feel good about it."

"Then it was a good trade," I concluded.

We are constantly trading in our lives. We're trading our time for things. We're trading our happiness for fear. We are trading watching TV for our health. We're trading a great marriage for pride. The list goes on and on. We're trading away knowledge every time we turn on music in our car instead of an audiobook or podcast. We're trading away memories for every family activity we miss or choose not to go on. We're trading away future money every time we use a credit card and pay interest on it. We're trading away an active life in our sixties and seventies if we choose to not exercise or eat healthily in our thirties and forties.

Who's to say what's a good trade or what's not?

I'm not going to give you my opinion on what I feel is a good trade or a bad trade. I think all our opinions are different. Just like boys trading pins, somebody who has the right information and the right knowledge and experience knows that you could get 10 or 12 pins for a particular pin. But because we don't have the right experience, knowledge, education, or maybe the willpower, we're willing to trade away great things of value for things that aren't so valuable.

What time are we trading away that is more valuable than what we are getting for it? What knowledge are we trading away to listen to the same song for the 100th time on the radio or listen to sports statistics that will be totally irrelevant in two weeks or two days? Are we trading away happiness because we were prideful, stubborn, or lazy? Are we trading away a better marriage we know is possible if we were more willing to put forth a bigger effort in pleasing our spouse? Are we trading away our dream of owning our own business for a false sense of security in the job that we're in now?

Be very aware that every choice, every decision that you make is a trade. We must be very conscious of what we are willing to trade away. Unlike the pins that Grayson traded that had no real value, the trades we make with our lives, our time, our money, our happiness, and our fulfillment are priceless. If we are not aware of what we are trading, we will end up on the short end of the stick on most of these trades.

I knew all the theories. I knew how trades worked, but at the time I felt like the day care centers were garbage pins that no one else wanted. Or worse, that my father-in-law and I had traded a coveted dinner plate pin for a couple of garbage pins.

Financially, it was a Hail Mary. The day care workers were set in their ways, not realizing that my strategy could get us to the end zone and start bringing in profits. We had to move the chains. We had to find the good in our "trade." We had to make our trade valuable. I had to turn six garbage pins into six dinner plates.

Chapter 21

Crab Cage

"Never dull your shine for someone else."

— **Tyra Banks**

*"Know your worth. Know the difference between what
you're getting and what you deserve."*

— **Anonymous**

We continued to work on the Bright Child Learning Centers to make them profitable. The centers were starting to do well, partially because I was completely immersed in operations this time around.

We had started to build a company culture of respect, honesty, and quality. The staff knew that I would do what I said I would do and I made sure they understood how I felt about them: that they, the staff, were the most important part of the company.

But after a year and a half of me running the centers, one of our directors quit and moved away, and I had to hire someone new. I had been working with Kathy Yoder, who had been involved with the company since day one and was our regional director when I took over. She had quickly become my right-hand woman. When I told her we needed to hire a new director, she suggested a friend she had known for eight or nine years. This friend had worked in the day care industry for 10 years. There was one problem. That friend was a man.

"I'm not hiring a man," I told her firmly. It may have been against the law to discriminate against men this way but men have a target on their back in the childcare industry. Parents aren't comfortable with men taking care of their kids. Day care work is a near-literal no man's land, and that was not just my option on the matter: Less than 3 percent of day care workers were male at the time I was looking for a director. Any man working in the day care industry was under constant suspicion.

I interviewed candidate after candidate but everyone was subpar. I didn't want to ruin all the progress we had made with a bad hire.

"Please just interview him," Kathy begged. She recited his resume and noted he was currently running a center for a national day care chain in Las Vegas.

"Kathy do you feel that strongly that we should hire this guy?" I asked

"A 110 percent yes," she said. "He is the best director I have ever worked with."

I relented. "Okay, bring him in for an interview"

His name was Cameron, and he blew me away. He knew the business. He was an expert on how to talk to parents and kids. He was very knowledgeable and knew how to run a center. He even explained the safeguards he put in place to protect himself as a male in the industry: He never changed diapers for infants. He communicated often with parents. He made sure he was never alone with children one on one. People at other centers who knew of him had nothing but great things to say about this candidate. It was almost too good to be true. Cameron checked all the boxes and it would have been a no-brainer to hire him if he had not been a man. Despite the fact that he was a man and I knew all the additional risks, I went against my gut and hired him to replace the director that was leaving.

In the months following the hire, I had a lot of meetings with Cameron. When we had director meetings with all six directors, he was by far the most capable of the group. Within a month, his center became one of the most improved centers. The problem with that center was it was twice as big as my other centers and had twice the rent. That meant you needed twice the enrollment to make it work. We were at half-capacity, and he continued to build as the economy slowly turned around. I was thoroughly impressed. On top of that, the staff loved him, and parents adored him.

Eventually, we were using all of the classrooms in his center and enrollment increased by 25 percent. Things were going well, and you could tell he was a major factor in the center's success. It looked like I was finally catching a break in this financial crisis. Maybe I could actually come out of this without being an utter failure.

Despite how hard I'd worked to get away from it, I was used to failure: it had plagued me since grade school.

On the last day of fourth grade, my classmates eagerly chattered around me, squawking like birds, and discussing their grades. I looked down at my own report card and my eyes focused in on the straight F staring back at me. I turned the paper over and saw that I wasn't going to move on to fifth grade. I would be repeating fourth grade.

It shouldn't have been surprising that every class had an "F" next to it. I had been absent more than 40 times that year. My home life was a disaster: Jim was creating chaos in our home almost every day as he came home drunk. I had three little brothers all under the age of four whom I helped care for, including nighttime feedings and diaper changing. My mom would rather me stay home and help her with the kids than to go to school, and I was more than willing to stay home: I hated school.

I missed two or three days every week. Most of the time I had no clue what they were talking about. That wasn't my only problem. Even when I was there for a few days in a row, I still couldn't keep up. I couldn't read, write, or spell. I couldn't read a word that had more than two syllables— forget about spelling words with more than three letters.

The next year, I was placed into special education classes to try and give me the extra help I needed. Jim went to jail again for a few months, so our home was as stable as it could be with four kids. I started not to hate school. I realized that I could do better if I went to school and actually tried to learn. Unfortunately, Jim was released from jail and our house fell back into the chaos that always followed him. But in special ed, I had realized that I could do okay at school if I just put my mind to it.

Years later, Jim was killed, and I moved in with my gram permanently. At Gram's, life was stable and I rarely missed a day of school. I started to realize that if I went to school and got some help that I could learn. My issue wasn't that I was stupid, it was that I wasn't putting in the time or effort to do well.

In seventh grade, a counselor from Penn State University came in to speak to us during an assembly. They talked about what you needed to do to get into college. As I sat there listening to the requirements, I thought about my situation, my future, and where would I be in a decade. Even though I was living with my gram, I still had to deal with being "that Tressler Boy." The one who dressed in hand-me-down clothes and every so often showed up with a bad haircut. The kid who couldn't read or write or spell. The kid who was in special ed and was so poor he got free lunch.

My life sucked. My future was looking more and more like I'd inherit a spot on the back of Uncle Bub's garbage truck, or at the very best, drive one of the garbage trucks.

In that moment, sitting on those hard assembly chairs, I realized I needed to do something to change the direction of my life. I needed to take control and do something that no Tressler had ever done. What if I could get a college degree? That would change my life. I wouldn't be stuck on the back of the garbage truck. Things could be different for me and my future family. A college degree would put me in a situation where my family wouldn't have to worry about opening the refrigerator door and only seeing half-used condiments. They wouldn't have to worry about not having money for everyday things.

I was excited for a split second until I looked at the reality of what that meant. A college degree? Of my mom's 15 brothers and sisters, only two had graduated from high school, and none had even attended a college. Of my 50 or so cousins, none had ever gone to college.

In my family, education was looked at as a necessary evil. Once you could find a job, you didn't need to go to school anymore. Pap didn't make it through the fourth grade before he dropped out of school to work on his family's farm. My gram made it through the fifth grade before she quit school to help raise her younger brothers and sisters. That tradition continued with my mom and her brothers and sisters. One by one, they dropped out of school either when they found a job or, in the case of most of the women, got pregnant.

What was I thinking? I would be lucky to graduate high school, let alone make it to college. As I sat there stewing, a weight of 1,000 pounds fell upon my shoulders as I realized what was ahead of me if I went after this goal. And then the voice started whispering all the reasons I shouldn't even be thinking such things. Nelson, you're in special ed, you can't read, you can't write, you can't spell, you have dyslexia.

You're a *Tressler*.

We all have that voice, the one in our brains that chimes up and recites a million reasons we shouldn't attempt anything new or different. You know the one, the one that tells us we're not good enough, smart enough, fast enough, pretty enough, rich enough. Sometimes it tells us to stay where we are. It tells us that what we are thinking is going to be hard and uncomfortable. It screams for us to stay put! You're safe here! Don't do anything out of the norm.

We have all heard that voice. That's the part of our brain that comes from our prehistoric ancestors. It's the part of the brain that wants to keep us comfortable.

But what was my choice, to stay in the situation I was in, to struggle through life just getting by? I was already hurting and uncomfortable. I had to do it. I had to get that degree. I had to change my future.

I left that auditorium with my first big goal and my first strong "why." I would be the first Tressler to get a college degree. The next day at school, I started to pay closer attention in class. I started to take notes as best I could, and I started to do the assignments that were assigned outside of class. I didn't suddenly turn into an "A" student. Yeah, far from it. I got mostly Cs, sprinkled with a B or two. But I could feel myself getting better. This improvement went on through the end of tenth grade. I was still going to special education classes.

We took a test in special ed every year that determined our progress. The day after taking it for sophomore year, I went back to the special education classroom, always careful not to be seen going in by anyone else. Ms. McCormick was there waiting for me. It looked like she had been crying but she had a smile on her face. I walked by her and sat at my chair at the table. She came and sat down next to me.

"Nelson, I want you to know how proud I am of you," she said. I looked at her in surprise.

"Okay, for what?"

"You will not be in my class or any other remedial classes next year. Your test scores were excellent, and you will no longer be in the special education program. Congratulations."

I was shocked. I felt like I was floating as I sat at that table hearing that news. She hugged me and again told me how proud she was of me as she started to cry. The next two years, I tried my best at school, and I even took a few college prep classes. I was still getting mostly Bs and Cs, but I did manage a few As, in PE and math. Fortunately, I had one other thing going for me: I was a pretty good athlete, and I was already getting some attention from a few colleges to come play football for them. Most liked what they saw on the field but stopped short when they saw my grades. But one school, St. Francis University in Pennsylvania, seemed willing to take a chance on me.

It should have been one of the most exciting times of my life and it was. But my family didn't understand.

Morning, Gram's house. Five or six people sitting around the kitchen table drinking coffee and catching up on the latest gossip before going to work. As I walked into the kitchen, I spotted a big 8 x 11 envelope sitting on the table. I glimpsed the St. Francis University emblem on the upper left-hand corner of the envelope. My name and Gram's address were typed neatly on the recipient label.

My heart fluttered in my chest. This was it. The envelope looked so prestigious and official. I had been waiting for this envelope for several weeks. I had applied to St. Francis University, having been to the school several times on football recruiting visits. St. Francis was a pretty good school, and despite my football invitation, acceptance was not a guarantee, especially with my grades.

I walked right up to the kitchen table and grabbed the envelope. My palms were sweating and my heart raced. I didn't have many options when it came to college. Whatever was in that envelope might make a huge difference in my life.

I took the envelope and walked into the living room so I could have some privacy as I opened it. I did not want my family to see me cry if I didn't get accepted: They were not above making fun of you during life's most vulnerable moments. Slowly, I ran my finger under the flap, breaking the adhesive in one fell swoop. I took a deep breath and pulled out the bright white letter.

"Congratulations…" That is the only word I remember reading. My heart leapt from my chest and a smile so big that it made my cheeks hurt spread across my face. I was going to be the first person in our family to go to college. Jobs that my aunts and uncles were working did not require any kind of education. They were working in the construction industry, cleaning houses, driving trucks, working on the back of a garbage truck. It was respectable work, but those weren't the careers I wanted for myself.

I composed myself and ran back into the kitchen to deliver my good news.

"I GOT ACCEPTED TO COLLEGE!" I said proudly, beaming from ear to ear.

Gram beamed back at me, pride shining in her eyes. She always told me that I was going to be something and do something with my life, and she could not have been prouder that I was now going to be able to go to college and start that journey of making something of myself.

Besides my gram, though, there were mixed emotions around the table. I knew there would be sarcasm. There was a "*Pooh,* college boy," or "They must be letting anyone in the college nowadays," or "What is your major going to be? Basket weaving?" I was prepared for the commentary, but what Aunt Miriam said to me was so unexpected that 30 years later I still can't forget it.

She was standing over by the window in the kitchen next to the trash can. I had paused in my celebration to eat, and when I finished breakfast, I walked over to clean off my plate into the garbage. Aunt Mariam stared out the window, avoiding eye contact with me. Suddenly, she said, "Do you think you're better than the rest of us now?"

I was stunned.

"No, I don't think I'm better than anybody. I just wanted to go to college and do something with my life," I replied. "I don't think I'm better than anybody," I said again, just in case she didn't hear me the first time.

I said this with an edge in my voice that clearly demonstrated I was unnerved by her question. She didn't say anything. She just turned her head and continued to look out the window. Maybe she felt some regret, thinking of opportunities lost and dreams that went unfulfilled in her own life.

Several of my cousins told me that I wouldn't last a year at college; that I would flunk out and be back in Coleville before too long. Others told me I would not have gotten into college without football.

The weeks following my acceptance into college were more of the same. Word quickly spread that I had been accepted, and everybody was more than willing to weigh in with their opinion of how things would work out. There were many hurtful things said to me as my family told me exactly what they thought.

"You can barely spell. How are you ever gonna make it in college?"

"You barely passed high school. How in the world did they let you into college?"

"Don't you have to be able to read to get in the college?"

"I've heard all you need is a pulse and a check to get into college nowadays. They better try cashing your check before they let you in."

These things were always said with a smile and a wink, but they still hurt worse than any physical injury I had ever had. I guess one of the advantages of being born into the Unlucky Sperm Club is that you grow up having very thick skin. I had heard these types of comments throughout my life, as I did things that nobody else in my family did.

It happened when I got my driver's license and got a new job. I quit working on my uncle's garbage truck, even though I'd worked on it since I was nine years old. I had earned about $50 a week since the time I could really pull my weight. The money had helped, but now that I had a driver's license, I could get a job outside of my family where I didn't have to be stuck in Coleville. And I could stop working for family, where it was okay to pay less than minimum wage.

While I was playing in one of my football games, Henry Haranin, the owner of a construction company, witnessed my drive and hustle. His son Scott was on my team.

"Nelson, let me talk to you a minute," he said, after our game had ended.

I couldn't imagine what he wanted with me, but I was curious.

"Listen, I'd like for you to work for me this summer," he said, "and I'd like you to take my son along with you, on jobs. I think he'd benefit from seeing your work ethic and your good attitude."

It was clear to Henry that Scott was living a cushioned life. The Haranins were some of the wealthiest people in Bellefonte. They owned a construction company that a few of my uncles worked for, and the company did a lot of work for Penn State. I think Henry wanted someone like me around his son so he would know how blessed he was.

I took the job that summer. It paid minimum wage in exchange for hot, physical work. One day, I decided to see if I could get a raise. I walked over to the construction trailer, parked off to the side of the construction site, and knocked on the sliding glass door. When Henry looked up from his desk, I slid the door open.

"Hey, Nelson! Come on in," he said, as he leaned back in his chair and tossed his pen onto a stack of papers on his desk. "What's up?"

I explained that I'd been doing a good job and that my work was consistently better than most. After I'd prefaced my request, I told him that I felt like I deserved a raise.

"Nelson, I'm paying you $3.71 an hour. If you can't make it on that, then I'll just have to use someone else," he said, without skipping a beat.

In less than four minutes, I was gone from his office and headed back to my work. But I felt like Henry respected me and the fact that I'd taken a chance and asked for a raise.

I didn't get a raise that day, but a year later, he set up a college scholarship fund and awarded the scholarship to me. It was for $1,000, and it helped a lot that first year of college. I am not sure if Henry knew that day I asked for a raise that he was going to set up this scholarship or not. But years later, I realized that if he had given me a raise on that day, his other high-school employees would have felt they also deserved a raise. The domino effect wouldn't have been good for the company. When he awarded me the college scholarship he'd funded, it was his way of helping me out. He knew my family situation, and he respected what I was doing despite where I came from. He saw that I wanted more for my life and that I was not willing to settle for the status quo.

I also think Henry also saw some big changes in his son, Scott, as we worked together. Scott realized how important a job could be to a 17-year-old. We had long conversations as we drove from construction site to construction site, and Scott's eyes were opened to a life he never knew existed: mine.

But each time I tried to grow and better myself, I was met with hurtful comments from my family. I later realized what was going on. It is called the crab mentality.

If you put one crab in a five-gallon bucket next to the sea, that crab will crawl out of the bucket and return to the sea. If you put multiple crabs in the bucket next to the sea, those crabs will all die in that bucket: When one crab attempts to climb out of the bucket, the other crabs quickly latch on to the one trying to escape and pull it back down. The crabs won't let others leave the bucket. If one crab repeatedly tries to get out of the bucket, the other crabs will break its legs. If that now disabled crab continues to persist, the other crabs will kill it. As bizarre as this may sound, humans have adopted this crab mentality. You saw how it played out in my family, but it happens everywhere.

People who find themselves stuck in the crab bucket must never allow what those other crabs are doing to be an excuse for them to fail. They can never look at the fact that everybody is trying to pull them back in as an excuse to give up and not try.

In my case, I used it as fuel every time things got hard. I would try even harder so that I could prove to the people who said I couldn't do it that not only could I do it but that I could do it better than anyone else.

There are crabs that make it out of the bucket. And, fortunately for me, I was one of them. Most of the time, that's where the crab mentality analogy stops. Crabs try to pull the escaping crabs back down and all the crabs die except the one who makes it out. But I feel like that's not the appropriate end to this life lesson. In fact, I feel like that should be just the beginning.

Once that crab has made it out of the bucket, he has been given a great gift. He is free to do whatever he wishes now that he doesn't have the other crabs constantly pulling him down. I think a lot of the crabs who escape want to head to the sea and never look back. Can you really blame them? But I think the crabs that get out of the buckets should head towards the sea and pursue their dreams and then return to the bucket to help the remaining crabs. Crabs that make it out can be an inspiration to the crabs that are still in the bucket. They can prove that anything is possible. They show the other crabs that there is a different path and different options and different outcomes.

Since I have escaped the crab bucket, I've had the opportunity to help and motivate others in my family to better themselves. I've had cousins attend and graduate college and trade schools. Many of my cousins participated and excelled in sports. Other cousins joined the armed forces. I'm not taking credit for their accomplishments, but I truly believe that after witnessing my success, others felt inspired to try the same.

The funny thing is now when I visit family back home, they are proud of me and treat me as if I'm a dignitary. I've been out of the Coleville crab bucket for 30 years. But the Tresslers are proud of this crab now. I don't think that the crab mentality means other crabs don't love you. It is just something that humans do, especially within families. I think a lot of times the people in our family who try to prevent us from going off and doing other things think they are trying to protect us. They feel that staying in the bucket keeps us from being hurt and disappointed.

Regardless of their intentions, we must not let others hold us back from pursuing our dreams or from escaping the circumstances that we were born into. Members of the Unlucky Sperm Club especially must fight and claw and pull ourselves out of situations that fate has put us in. The fact that fate has put us into these circumstances is one of the reasons we can climb out of the crab bucket. We can use those circumstances to strengthen us. Our struggle becomes our fuel. No amount of pulling by other crabs will hold us down.

Even while we're in the bucket, we need to be listening for the waves of sea just outside our view. We need to hear those waves breaking on the shore. We do this by filling our bodies and our minds with good things that will help us grow mentally, physically, spiritually, and emotionally. As we hear those waves breaking on the shoreline, we should allow the sounds to be an alarm, telling us to get up and get out of that bucket.

Use that strength fostered from your experiences as motivation to propel yourself not only out of the bucket but to places that people in the bucket have never even considered going. Once you have gone to those places, return to the bucket and help the other crabs left behind so that they can pursue their own dreams. They know it can be done because of your example, and they will succeed with your support.

While the financial crisis persisted and the news continued its coverage of the child molester, it seemed I was being pulled back to the bottom every time I tried to get out of this mess. I knew I had to keep trying. Just as the crabs could hear those waves breaking on the shore, I knew I would eventually make it out of the bucket if I just kept trying.

Chapter 22

Up, Up, and Away

"Your wings already exist. All you have to do is fly."

— Anonymous

Early in our relationship, like countless other couples, Skye and I went Christmas shopping together. I'd never been much of a shopper or a great gift-giver. It just wasn't an area in which I excelled. I tried to think of something that Skye might like, a gift that said I'd thought of her with some consideration.

Gram had always kept her house especially cold, not out of preference but out of necessity. It had been a matter of economics. Heat cost money. It was less expensive for us to bundle up than it was for Gram to pay to heat her house. So all the way through ninth grade I wore long, flannel, footed pajamas that zipped up the front. They were cozy, comfortable, and warm. As I grew taller, I just cut off the feet of my pajamas and then wore socks on my feet.

That's it! I decided. *Footie pajamas! Skye will love them!*

While she and I were out shopping at the local mall, I found some footed pajamas and I told her the story of how we'd all worn them as kids in Gram's house. She seemed to understand the warmth behind my childhood memories and the sentiment that was behind my story of how we wore them to bed each night.

"I love that story. They're cute!" she agreed, cementing my belief that she indeed needed a pair for herself.

Skye busied herself in some other part of the department store and I went back and purchased a set of red footie pajamas. I was sure that she'd love them as much as I once had.

When we exchanged Christmas gifts, I was overwhelmed to see all the thoughtful gifts Skye had bought for me. A watch, a few nice shirts, and a stocking stuffed with all the sweets and snacks that I loved. She must have paid attention to everything I ever said when it came to what I liked. When I gave her the red pajamas, she politely feigned sheer delight and thanked me with a big hug and a kiss. It would be some time before I'd realize that it was her proper upbringing that had allowed Skye to summon her manners and thank me for my gift. Those red footie pajamas would become fodder for future jokes, right along with the sweater vest that only I love. But at the time, I was still finding my way, testing the waters, and figuring out how and where I fit into the world.

Now as I wondered whether our marriage would last, I would do anything to hear Skye laugh again. I hurt. She hurt. And footie pajamas were not going to fix our marriage. Neither were good manners and polite acceptances. I was treading water. In terms of business, the day cares were okay. Doggie District still had dogs coming to stay. The economy was stagnant and real estate deals remained elusive. Things were not getting much better but in a way, they were not getting worse.

Our boys continued with their lives, assuming I was just busy with work. Skye and I were at a stalemate. I did not want to lose her, or my family, or all the things I had worked so hard for. I wish I could apply for a reprieve. Marriage is hard. It isn't just about being in love; it's about all the other things that go along with being married. Raising kids, paying bills, working through disagreements. If it was just about being in love, it would be simple.

That's true for many things in life. If college was just about playing football and none of the other stuff, it would have been simple. But there was a lot more to my journey through higher education, and I knew there'd be a lot more to fixing my marriage.

Even though I had received some scholarship money, I learned there would be expenses, fees, and additional costs to pay. St. Francis is three hours from Bellefonte, so I had to move to campus. My coaches told me not to worry about the money because I could apply for financial aid. This entire world was foreign to me, so I took their word for it.

I found that if I filled out dozens of forms, I would be considered for extra financial assistance. I had saved some money from my garbage truck work and construction job, but I knew it would never be enough.

"Hey, Gram," I said, as she stirred a pot at the stove, "What's your annual income?"

"Well now, let me think a minute. I guess it'd be $4,800."

"Forty-eight *hundred*?" I repeated. "A *year*?"

"Yes, that's right."

"Oh. Uh, okay."

My breath caught as I digested that very small sum and wondered how Gram possibly could make ends meet on $4,800 a year. Life was expensive.

After completing my applications, I received some grants like the federal Pell grant and others. I reported for football practice and began my college classes that fall. I felt like I was on the cusp of the next stage of my life. But by the end of the first semester, I got a bill from the school saying I owed an additional $1,000. By the end of the second semester, I received another bill for $3,500. In addition to the debt, I also had acquired a broken nose and a broken elbow, compliments of football.

I couldn't afford to keep going to college. When I went home that first summer between classes, I sat with Gram on her front porch swing.

"You know, I'm proud of you," Gram said. "I'm proud that you're studying and working on a college degree."

I sighed and hesitated to tell her what I'd been thinking.

"Yeah, well, I don't think I can afford college. It's a lot more expensive than I'd thought. I was able to pay the $1,000 after the first semester, but I've got another bill for $3,500, and I just don't have it."

Tears welled up in my eyes. I had come so far, but once again I felt life was dealing me a less-than-desirable hand.

Uncle Bub offered to pay the $3,500. I was touched, but I knew that was a stretch for him. I couldn't accept the money. Besides, it would only cover one semester. I'd be right back in the same position the following semester.

"So what're you planning to do?" Gram asked me.

I had a plan. "Rusty, one of my buddies, is going into the Air Force. He said he can set me up with a recruiter he knows and that I'll be able to go to college while I'm in the Air Force. It sounds like my best option."

A few weeks later the recruiter signed me up and I was enlisted in no time. I knew I would miss wearing No. 48 on my St. Francis football jersey but it was time to move on. When I said goodbye to my family, Gram was in tears. It was one of the only times I'd ever seen her cry. It pained me, too, to leave, but I also knew that it was the only way I'd ever truly leave Bellefonte.

For me, the Air Force checked all the boxes. I'd learn applicable and marketable skills, I'd get a college education, and I'd get out of Bellefonte. The future was ripe with opportunity and I was eager to liberate myself. It was fear that drove me: I couldn't bear to think that I might always work on the garbage truck and build a life in the small town of my birth, the very place that had overshadowed my entire existence.

Nervous but excited, I plunged into my plan. When I boarded the plane for basic training in Texas, bound for my future, it was the first time ever that I'd been on an airplane. But an hour later, as I looked out at the clouds, I realized, "I could be anything and anyone in the world that I wanted to be."

Joining the Air Force gave me another fresh start. Like it was when I started college, no one knew my history, my family, or the black mark that hung over the Tressler name. It was as if someone had kindly erased it all and removed the shackles that had bound me for decades. I was finally Nelson Nobody.

Basic training wasn't bad.

I was in good physical shape thanks to football, but I found that in the Air Force, the challenges were more mental than physical. Discipline was at the forefront of all we did. Coat hangers had to be spaced precisely two inches apart, shoes had to be spit-polished, grooming was critical, and even beds had to be made with near-computer precision. I fell in line and followed the rules.

New recruits quickly learned of the infamous "Texas Tornadoes," the dreaded 3:00 a.m. wakeups that occurred when the drill sergeants burst in and tossed all our belongings. Satisfied with their destruction, and the fact that we'd be up until dawn cleaning and organizing, the tornadoes moved on.

"Clean this crap up!" they'd yell, and then they'd leave to go back to sleep, laughing at you.

This was new to some of the guys. I, however, had lived through Jim. He, too, would come home at 3:00 a.m., wake everyone up by screaming and breaking things. But unlike the drill sergeants, Jim was not forbidden from physically touching the people he woke up. That being the case, I had no problem with the 3:00 a.m. "Texas Tornadoes."

I sailed through basic training. Months later, it was Christmastime, and I felt homesick. The tech schools closed down during the Christmas holiday, so any student who wanted to was allowed to go home for two weeks. I jumped at this opportunity and flew home to see my family. I wanted to surprise my gram.

I had never not seen her for Christmas. We spoke earlier on a call and she told me how sad she was she couldn't see me this year.

"But you are where you are supposed to be. You're going to make something out of your life, Nelson," she told me for the thousandth time.

I loved it when she said that. Two thousand miles away from Coleville, I was starting to believe it. I told my mom that I was coming home and that I wanted to surprise Gram. She loved the idea and knew just how to do it.

On Christmas morning, all our family gathered at Gram's house. A gigantic refrigerator box sat on her front porch near the porch swing atop the scuffed flooring that had been worn down from thousands of hours of swinging and talking.

"Gram, look!" someone said. "Nelson sent you something for Christmas! Go out and see what it is!"

As soon as I heard the familiar squeak of her door, I popped out of the box and surprised her.

"Merry Christmas, Gram!" I said, and she hurried over to me, happier than I'd seen her in a long time.

The Air Force seemed to be a good fit for me. I liked the routine, the opportunity to learn new things, and the fact that I was growing as a person. But I wasn't the only one who'd made some changes and better choices in life. My mom was doing great too. She'd been with Pat for nine years by then and she was very happy. You could really see my mom starting to grow into a wonderful person now that she was safe from all the terror that Jim had put her through.

While I was going to St. Francis that first year of college, Pat would sometimes give me a hundred dollars and joke, "There's my child support!" I loved hearing him say it, as much as I thought he enjoyed reminding us both that we were indeed "father and son." Pat always treated my brothers the same too. He couldn't have been any more a father to us if we'd shared the same genetics. In fact, we eventually forgot that we weren't biologically related. To us, Pat was our father just the same as if we really did share

DNA. When I left for the Air Force, I was so glad to know that Mom was being treated well and that life was finally looking up for her.

Mom and Pat had shown me it was possible for life to get better. I hoped Skye and I could turn things around and build an even stronger life together. If we couldn't, how long would it be until I was paying child support? If the economy kept going the way it was going, I would be lucky if I could afford to pay the same couple of hundred dollars that Pat had given me years earlier.

Chapter 23

Like Father, Like Son

"Those who don't move don't notice the chains."

— **Rosa Luxemburg**

After a particularly stressful day, I came home exhausted and frustrated. As I walked through the door, I noticed that Dawson, who was 13 at the time, had made a mess in the living room. Half-eaten yogurts, bags of chips, and barely touched bottles of Gatorade lay scattered from one end of the room to the other. Toys, clothes, and shoes covered the rest of the floor. I asked him to clean it up and take his stuff up to his room, but he just looked up at me and then turned his attention back to the TV. He was at that age of defiance, seeing how far he could push boundaries. I couldn't ask Skye to intervene because we were barely on speaking terms. It seemed like every time we opened our mouths, the word "divorce" came flying from our lips.

"Dawson, clean up the living room before dinner," I told him once more. I walked into the kitchen for a drink of water. When I returned to the living room, Dawson still had not followed instructions. In that moment, I felt boiling anger travel from my toes to my ears. "Dawson, I said now."

"I will when I'm done. What's up your butt, Dad?"

It happened so quickly. I walked over to Dawson, grabbed him by the shirt, and threw him up the stairs. He stumbled and I towered over him again and again, lifting him by the shirt collar until I pushed him up the stairs and right into his room. I threw him onto the bed, still cuffing the collar of his shirt.

"Be quiet and do what I say! I am sick of you talking back to me!"

In that moment, the past slapped me hard, as a flashback of Jim towering over me washed over me. I broke out into a cold sweat, loosening my grip on Dawson's shirt. *What on earth am I doing?* I let him go, looking down into his confused eyes. He was scared; he had never seen me like this before. By this time, Branson and Grayson were crying, too, not knowing what was going on. I slowly walked out of Dawson's room and down the stairs. Skye was coming up the stairs in a panic, thinking that something had happened to one of the boys. I felt immensely guilty. It was one of the scariest moments of my life. I had become exactly what I hated. Like "father," like son.

I was 12 years old. Jim and my mom were in the middle of a full-fledged fistfight. My mom was throwing anything that she could get her hands on at Jim, hitting him with about half of the stuff she threw. Jim was drunk, so he was not feeling the full effect of the arsenal. I was asleep in my room when the screams woke me. I ran down the stairs and stood at the bottom. Soon my mom ran out of things to throw at Jim and he closed the distance between them in three or four giant steps, pouncing on her and punching her in the face with all of his strength. She tried to fend off the blows by bringing her arms in front of her face, but Jim fists barely slowed down as punch after punch connected.

I started to scream and yell as loud as I could for him to stop, but he was in a rage—he didn't know what was going on around him. I ran over and grabbed him by the neck in a headlock. I squeezed as hard as my 12-year-old arms could squeeze. This broke his trance, and he turned his attention to me. He straightened up, with me still wrapped around his neck. He pulled my arms open and broke my grip, and tossed me across the room like a sack of potatoes. I hit the floor flat on my back, the breath knocked out of me. I struggled to move, fearing that he was coming after me to finish what he had started. Instead, he staggered across the room and headed up the stairs to his bed.

I crawled over to my mom to see if she was okay. Her face was unrecognizable; she had blood coming out of her nose and mouth. Her eyes were already swollen. She was crying, trying to catch her breath—Jim had broken a few ribs. I hugged her and we cried as we laid on the floor together.

I would never forget that night, and yet—had I just done the same thing to my kids? Would this be a memory that they never forgot? Would they judge me based on this?

Piece by piece everything around me was breaking. My career, my marriage, and now my entire family.

Chapter 24

How Did I Get Here?

"If you ever ask yourself: How did I get here? It probably means that you are living a life worth living."

— Isador

When I was in the Air Force, I worked on an aircraft called the EF-111 Raven. It's a sophisticated aircraft that was created to replace the B-66 destroyer used by the US Air Force. It had no guns or missiles or any other weapons, yet it was deployed on every major air offensive that the US launched during its use. The closest thing it had to any fire power was a few anti-missile chaff-and-flares that the pilots could use if they were fired upon.

Even so, this aircraft was considered one of the deadliest planes in the US arsenal. The Ravens were considered a clear and present danger because of what they did to enemy communications and their ability to see what was coming: It was an electronic jamming airplane. It would go in front of the bombers and fighter aircraft and unleash its jamming devices. The EF-111s were so powerful that three of these aircraft had the combined capability to jam all electronic communications on the entire east coast of the US. Any aircraft "hit" by the EF-111s power had no clue what was coming or where it was coming from. All they would see on their screens, and heard on their devices, was pure static. While the enemy scrambled to get their bearings, more US aircraft were coming behind the EF-111s. With the enemy blinded and not able to communicate, the large bombers and fighter aircraft could easily come and destroy their desired targets.

You can see how dangerous these planes were, since they effectively blinded the enemy. How could the enemy be expected to defend themselves when they had no clue what was happening and once it happed where it came from?

Although most of us will never be under attack by large bombers or fighter aircraft, we're still walking through life blanketed by static. We don't know where things are coming from or what to even to look for. We are preoccupied with so many things and distractions that don't matter, and are blind and deaf to the possibilities that can make huge differences in our lives for better or for worse.

I mustered out of the Air Force and was completing my senior year of college at UNLV, which was the fourth university I attended—life in the Air Force moves you around quite a bit. I was married to Skye and we had had our first child, Dawson. I was pursuing my degree in business with an emphasis on finance. I had planned on being an investment banker or a stockbroker. But then I met with my counselor to ensure that I had all the requirements to graduate and was shocked to learn I needed an internship. He gave me a list of three or four companies which had offered internships in the past, and I called to see if they had any available.

The first two companies on the list were stockbroker companies. Neither offered internships at the time but told me to call back next semester.

Then I called an investment banker and fortunately for me, they had an internship available. The first interview went well. They called me back and asked me to come for a second interview with the owner of the company.

"Bring a writing sample with you," they told me before hanging up the phone. *Oh no.* I was applying to be an investment banker, not an English teacher. With my dyslexia, I was lucky Skye had helped me with all my

English papers up to this point. She was good too: I got As on all of them. I decided to take along one of those papers.

The interview with the owner of the company went well. I was 27 years old, had been through four years of the military, and owned my own window-cleaning business. They could see my work ethic was there and my grades were pretty good. I had a good attitude and was willing to put forth the effort to be successful. At the end of the interview, they asked me for my writing sample. I slid it across the conference room table.

The owner picked it up and read over the paper during the next five minutes. Then he looked up.

"Do you have another writing sample?" he asked.

I told him I did not have another one but I could provide one. He said good because if this was the only writing sample I had that I would not get the job.

"How so? I received an A on this paper," I said.

He explained what was wrong with the paper and why writing was so important to an investment banker. I can't remember much of what he said. My brain was swimming, knowing that there was no way I was ever going to make it in the industry if it required lots of writing.

The next day, I went back to meet with my counselor and let him know that I had not had any luck with finding an internship. He broke out another list of the businesses that had hosted interns in previous years. Even though they didn't have current internships listed, they might have something available if I called.

I called the companies on the list. There were eight or 10 of them in all kinds of different fields and businesses. Most weren't looking for interns. I finally got a maybe from a commercial real estate company. I had no clue what commercial real estate was. But they said that they had one agent who might be offering an internship. They gave me Michael Kammerling's phone number.

I remember calling him three times that first week. If I didn't get an internship, I would have to wait another semester to get my diploma. This was not an option: Our son Dawson was already a year or so old. I had started the window cleaning business when I began going to UNLV and made about $7,000 a year. Fortunately, Skye worked at her father's dental practice as a dental assistant and Skye's mom, Marla, was kind enough to babysit Dawson for free. We even lived with Skye's parents and two of her brothers, Austin and Landon, for a year when I first got out of the Air Force while we tried to save enough money for our own place. I needed to graduate and get a job.

After four more calls, Michael Kammerling took my call, and he *was* looking for an intern. He told me to come in that week for an interview. I was excited, even though I had no idea what this internship would entail or even what commercial real estate really was.

Michael was an intimidating person. He was in his late forties at the time and I'd read that he was the top-producing broker at that firm. You could tell he bought his clothes somewhere other than Walmart or even Target. When I sat across from him at the conference room table, I was so nervous and intimidated that I felt like I was having an out-of-body experience.

I can't remember what questions he asked me or what answers I gave him, but I do remember he commented on my wardrobe. He said if I got the internship, I'd need to buy nicer clothes. I was recently married. I had a one-year-old child and was washing windows to make ends meet. I remember thinking, *Oh man, these are the nicest clothes I have.* Michael told me he would call me in a couple of days to let me know about the internship. I waited a week and heard nothing. I called to follow up but got his voicemail. I called the next day and was put through to his voicemail again. I called the following day and left another voicemail. I'm not sure he understood how important this internship was to me. But I needed this internship, and I was not going to go away quietly. After my fifth call with no answer, I took it upon myself to go back into his office and ask for him in person.

It was 112 degrees that day and I had been outside washing windows in Las Vegas. The windows were so hot that the water that you put on them would dry within seconds, barely giving you enough time to squeegee. It was brutal work, and this increased my determination to go into the office for my impromptu appointment. Fortunately, Michael was in and decided to see me. I told him I was in the area and wanted to make sure of my start date so I could plan accordingly. He chuckled—knowing that he had ignored my calls. I'm not sure if he planned on hiring me but I think he saw what type of work ethic and determination I had. He also realized that those were the type of characteristics that made a good salesperson. He told me I could start the following Monday.

I shook his hand with a big smile on my face and thanked him. As I walked out the door, he called my name and said, "Remember what I told you about your clothes. Go out and get yourself something nice." It didn't matter that I had no idea how I was going to be able to afford nice clothes. I had the internship and I would figure out a way.

I learned that the internship involved some writing, which scared me to death. We had to write letters of intent. These were offers to lease properties that had the main deal points outlined. This was not the formal contract or the lease but just 17 or 18 of the main deal points to ensure that there was a deal to be made. Fortunately for me, we use the same LOI every time, and all I had to do was input different names and different terms depending on what deal we were working on. I was able to fake it well enough. I was also responsible for doing the brochures for the properties Michael was marketing for landlords.

I did better on the phone with clients than I did writing LOIs or marketing brochures. Michael was very busy working on big deals that would pay huge commissions, but there were always calls coming through from smaller tenants looking for smaller spaces and Michael did not want to deal with them. The smaller deals needed to be handled and addressed, otherwise, he would lose the listings on these properties that turned into sales and bigger commissions. I started to take these calls for Michael. I had a knack for dealing with the smaller business owners.

Michael was from New York, and if you've ever dealt with a New Yorker, you know they are no-nonsense people. But even Michael was impressed with what I was doing with the smaller tenants. I sat right outside his office, so I overheard him talking to the landlords that he was leasing space for in their shopping centers. The landlords told him what a good job he was doing filling up their shopping centers. They didn't know it was me making the cold calls to bring in the deals but Michael knew it was me getting these deals done.

Then I started making cold calls to tenants out of the Yellow Pages. We called it dialing for dollars. Most people hate to cold call—it usually ends with somebody hanging up on you or yelling at you for disturbing them at their business. But I would play games with myself. By the time I had cold-called a lot, I realized it took me about 20 noes to get a yes. I started keeping track of the noes and was happy every time I got one because I knew as soon as I got around 20 that the yes was coming. Almost like magic, after the 20th no, on the 21st I would hear a yes.

Then something even more magical happened. After a few weeks of cold calling it was only 15 noes until I got a yes. Then 10 noes until I got a yes, as I worked on my presentation on the phone and started analyzing what worked and what didn't work. Eventually, I got down to about seven for every yes. Michael was impressed.

That internship gave me the last piece of the puzzle I needed to finally have all the requirements to get my college degree. It had been 12 years, four different colleges and four years in the Air Force. It was one of the sweetest moments of my life as I walked across that stage to accept my diploma. But it couldn't be bested by the moment I walked outside to see Skye and her family. They had a special surprise waiting for me. Standing next to Skye were my mom and Pat! Skye had arranged for them to come from Pennsylvania to be at my graduation as a surprise. The smile on my mom's and Pat's faces is, to this day, one of the best things I have ever seen.

Graduating was not just a goal that belonged to me. I had worked hard to get this degree but so had so many other people. Skye had worked full time at the dental office to give me time to go to school. Her dad gave her a job, her mom watched Dawson for free, and her brothers shared their home. Pat had given my mom and brothers a safe and secure life so I didn't have to worry anymore for their safety and well-being. My mom had given me everything she could over the years. My gram had given me support and encouragement my entire life. Chuck and Mary and their families had given me contrast. The people who had helped me achieve this goal were many. This was not just me fulfilling this goal, it was a long list of people that had given me so much in so many ways.

It was soon after that day that Michael offered me a job as his full-time assistant. He could see I had a knack for this business. I could deal with his temper and hard demeanor and not be offended whenever he yelled at the top of his lungs at me for screwing something up. And anyway, I loved the work. I accepted the job quickly. I still washed windows after work and on the weekends because I was only making $9 an hour with Michael. The agreement was that I would work and be paid $9 an hour for the first year before I could collect commissions on the deals that I closed.

That internship changed my life. It was a tough business. Being a middleman is not easy. You're constantly trying to help two opposing minds meet. Typically, you were dealing with two very strong personalities, one a business owner and the other a landlord. And for some reason, they both prided themselves on being shrewd negotiators. I quickly realized why burnout was such a common occurrence in commercial real estate.

I continued to work with Michael for the next five years until I went out on my own. By this time, Michael and I, as a team, had been the number one Grubb & Ellis team in the world three of the previous four years. But I wanted to have my own team and do things my way. Michael had taught me a lot about what to do and what not to do. I wanted to see what I could do on my own. In 2006, I started my own team. I was scared out of my mind. Was I really going to walk away from a situation that was working so well? One which had paid me more money than I could have ever imagined earning? Why in the world would I ever do anything to disrupt what I had created?

When I first started working for Michael, I couldn't help but notice the big deals he would get. The first big check that I remember was for $7,000. I imagined what my life could be if I were able to get checks like that someday. I had worked the year before cleaning windows in Las Vegas in 118-degree heat and made $7,200 total. Michael had that in one check on the corner of his desk.

That night, I went home and told Skye about the check Michael got. We laid in bed that night and dreamed of the things that we would do with that kind of money. It was so fun. We thought all our troubles would be over with a $7,000 check.

But there were no daydreams that could take my thoughts away from the trouble that Skye and I were in now, not to mention the trouble our day care centers were in.

Chapter 25

When Religion Comes A-Knocking

"No pain that we suffer, no trial that we experience is wasted."

— Orson F. Whitney

"Please, please help me. If not me, help my family; help the people who work with me. Help!" I cried out from my knees in a much-overdue prayer. Until this point, I had felt unworthy of asking that I be spared the misery being piled upon me when so many other good people were not being spared, not even a little bit. How could I ask for help to save my stuff?

I felt unworthy of help anyhow, considering where I came from. I mean—come on, I am a member of The Unlucky Sperm Club and the universe was obviously here to make things right again and put me back in my place. I was shocked it had taken this long. Could I really ask God to stop that?

I wanted to hide from everyone and everything at this time, just like when I was a kid avoiding things that I didn't understand or want to deal with. Back then, I could ignore a problem and it would just literally go away.

It was like that time when my Aunt Sue, who lived at the top of the dead-end street, called to let us know that the Jehovah's Witnesses had just left her house. We could see them just walking off the porch as Roseann, who'd taken Sue's phone call, passed on the alert.

They were two portly women in denim skirts, and they were eyeballing my gram's house with its porch full of people. There are military drills that were not as rehearsed as what people did on my gram's porch when the Jehovah's Witnesses threatened. Everybody sprang into action. My Aunt Roseann just kept walking after she gave us the news, like she was doing a drive-by.

My Aunt Connie, who lived directly across the street from Gram, quickly shot up, grabbed two-year-old Gloria by the wrist, and almost skipped across the road to her house to fortify it against these noble adversaries. Aunt Darlene, who lived in the trailer behind Gram, was stealthier. She almost crawled out of her seat, using the flower beds as cover, as she made her way back to her house. My Aunts Miriam and Sandy, who lived further down the dead-end street, worked in tandem, one keeping an eye out as the other moved off the porch, both issuing commands at each other under their breath. They followed my Aunt Darlene to the back of Gram's house and then made their way to their homes via a secret trail through the backyards.

Gram, me, and my cousin, John, went through the front screen door, and then Gram barked orders to shut the front door and pull down the blinds. All of this took place in a matter of seconds. I wish someone had timed us. What once was a bustling front porch noisy with chatter about the day's gossip and comments on the two or three cars that went up and down the street was now an abandoned ghost town. The vacant swing rocked back and forth in the breeze.

Knock. Knock.

Gram, as she always did while hiding behind a chair, motioned with her hands in a quick vertical fashion, up and down, signaling to John and me to stay belly-down by the chair we were hiding behind. You would've sworn these two women in their denim skirts carried the bubonic plague—we barely breathed, let alone let out any kind of sound.

But these two women knew this porch had been filled with eight or so people just seconds before. This was not their first rodeo.

After one more series of knocks on our front door, they walked around the sidewalk to the back door. But this was not our first rodeo either. One time, we hid in the kitchen that had a window to the sidewalk and the denim-skirt sisters saw us sitting at the kitchen table. That was the reason we were hiding behind the living room couch and chair. These women were not going to outsmart the Tresslers. We could hear their slow, methodical knocks at our back door and our hearts raced. It was as if we thought they had a battering ram and were mere seconds away from attack. These women would teach us their religion whether we wanted it or not.

But this time, the suspense was too much for John and me. That or maybe it was the fact that John had just farted the quietest fart in the world. It was one of those farts where it is just the sound of air being released into the wild. I started to laugh. Then John started to laugh, and Gram went into Navy SEAL mode, commando-crawling over to where John and I were. She clapped her hands over our mouths, trying to stifle the sound. This only increased the volume and the intensity. Before long, we were laughing harder than we had ever laughed before and we knew the jig was up.

The two women finally left our house and made their rounds knocking on all the doors on my gram's street. Nobody answered except for my Uncle Ralph, two doors down from us. He would politely answer the door, let the women get out their speech and then, in a matter-of-fact tone, tell them to, "Go sell crazy somewhere else."

This scenario played itself out at least three or four times each year, and every time it played itself out, everybody got a little bit better at avoiding the denim-skirt sisters.

As you can tell, religion was not a big part of my family's life. We weren't even Christmas-and-Easter religious. Coleville had a small church, and 20 to 25 people attended it each Sunday, but none of those were members of my family. However, once in a while, the church would have a special event where all the kids would go to make arts and crafts. We got treats. The attendance shot up to about 75 or 80 on these days because all the Tressler kids would go for a free snack and activity. But the church eventually realized there was much more work than it was worth: having 50 Tressler kids in the same building at the same time never boded well for the people in charge of the building.

That was it for religion, except for a few visits with one of the girl-friends I had in high school. And I attended services during basic training because it got me out of the bunkhouse for two or three hours a week. I had no clue what religion I was so I went to the nondenominational services. I can remember enjoying the singing and then feeling the guilt as the pastor preached hellfire and damnation upon us for all the sins that we had committed. After that, I did not have any desire to attend any organized religion services.

I believed in God, as did all the Tresslers. We just didn't live the teachings or adhere to the values and the standards that were taught, mainly because we didn't know what those were. It was almost as if God had left us alone, and we were going to leave him alone, so we both could go on our merry way.

That strategy worked until I met Skye and we decided to get married.

This is where all the sirens and the flashing warning lights are going off in this book because I am going to talk about organized religion. I know there are many people out there who feel like there is no place in their life for organized religion. Remember, we fled the front porch and took cover in our bunkers trying to stay away from the denim-skirt sisters. But I cannot in good conscience write this book and leave out such a big part of what helped me deal with my membership in the Unlucky Sperm Club. That is my disclaimer—now I'll proceed with my story.

It was the National Finals Rodeo in Las Vegas, and I was on temporary duty at Nellis Air Force Base. I'd been there for about 60 days when some guys in my squadron decided to go to a country western bar called Dylan's. With the rodeo in town, it was sure to be hopping, and they had a

$15 all-you-could-drink mug deal. Me and the guys in my squadron were going to put this bar out of business if they were only charging $15 for all we could drink.

Garth Brooks and Alan Jackson were at the peak of their careers. So I put on a pair of cowboy boots and a flannel shirt, getting as close to cowboy as I could. (Redneck, hick, white trash, hillbilly, and backwards country folk were all terms that had been used to describe my family and me but cowboy was still a stretch.)

We headed off to Dylan's to find me a cowgirl. And it was love at first sight. Full disclosure, my sight was a bit blurry when I saw Skye walking off the dance floor. But my vision was clear enough to see the most beautiful eyes I had ever seen and the prettiest smile ever smiled.

"Where have you been all night?" I asked her with my smooth operator line. What girl could resist a line like that? She rolled her eyes. That didn't deter me. I began to follow her around like a lost puppy. She was there with two friends from her work as a legal secretary at a law firm. We ended up dancing a few dances, probably out of pity because I would not leave her alone.

The guys from my squadron left me at the bar. They warned me that they were leaving but I wasn't going to let Skye out of my sight. Fortunately for me, Skye and her friends were willing to give me a ride to my hotel. They sat me in the backseat all by myself. I'm not sure if they were afraid of a strange man in their car or they wanted nothing more to do with me. But I was not giving up that easy. I reached around to the front seat and started to give Skye a neck rub, thanking her for the fun night. It worked. We exchanged numbers and shockingly enough, she called me the next day.

We spent every moment we could together over the next two and a half weeks before I had to go back to New Mexico, where I was stationed at Clovis Air Force Base. She was unlike any girl I'd ever met before. Brutally honest, sensitive, sweet, no-nonsense, and yet quick to laugh over absolutely nothing. As we got to know each other, it came to light that Skye had snuck into the bar without an ID. She was only 18 years old, and I was 22. On her eighteenth birthday, she'd moved out of her parent's house into an apartment with five or six of her friends. Her family was very religious, and Skye had adopted a lifestyle that did not align with her family's standards and values. You know, like sneaking into a bar at the age of 18 and driving home strange men at two in the morning. I had no idea that she was that young.

I was already head-over-heels for her. We talked every night by phone. The next thing I knew, I was in a car driving 12 hours back to Las Vegas so that I could spend the weekend with her. It was at this time that I got to meet her family. Skye trained me like I was a presidential candidate making his first big debate appearance: I swore like a sailor and drank like a fish, and neither one of those would've been acceptable to Skye's family. "Don't swear. My family doesn't swear. And don't order any alcohol. My family doesn't drink at all," she told me.

She had me scared to death to do anything in front of her family. Was it okay to breathe? They sounded like a bunch of religious zealots, especially considering the family that I had come from.

We met at a Mexican restaurant and I was on my best behavior; dressed in my best sweater vest. I was as nervous as a cat in a room full of rocking chairs. Her family seemed so happy and nice. Her stepfather reminded me of Ned Flanders on *The Simpsons*: He had the same mustache and was so happy. I'm sure it didn't hurt that Skye had practically prepared me to meet the Pope. The dinner ended up going well and I didn't feel like I embarrassed Skye or myself too much. I went back to New Mexico and we continued our long-distance relationship until October.

We were in love. I went out to Vegas again for Skye's cousin's wedding. Thoughts and emotions ran through us both. These feelings were ones I never thought I'd experience. I decided I wanted to spend the rest of my life with her. I proposed to her in her apartment that weekend, on one knee, just like in the movies.

The wedding was set for January in Las Vegas. We got married in a traditional church. There was no alcohol at the reception, which blew my family away. A wedding reception without alcohol made absolutely no sense to any of them. If they would've known that, they wouldn't have made the 32-hour van ride to attend. The meshing of Skye's and my family was a huge concern for me. Her family was professional, religious, and proper. My family, not so much. I was constantly telling them to stop swearing and to not do things that I knew Skye's family not only found weird but offensive. On my wedding day, I was more nervous about what my family was doing than I was about getting married to Skye.

Skye and I had only been together a handful of times before our wedding because we lived so far apart. We moved back to New Mexico with nine months until my enlistment was up, and we had a lot of learning ahead of us, about how to be married *and* about each other.

Let me describe Clovis, New Mexico, for you. It is a farming town that has been lost in time. It had the Air Force Base, a Walmart, and a Red Lobster that was open Thursday through Sunday only. The biggest excitement for the kids of this town was to go down on Main Street and cruise back and forth, just like they did back in the '50s. It was voted the worst Air Force Base in the world, although I don't think that was official. But it was certainly not on anybody's top list of assignments in the Air Force.

Skye had lived in Las Vegas, one of the most exciting cities in the world. It has more entertainment options than potato chips have varieties. Couple that with the fact that our first apartment was so small that you could literally go to the bathroom, watch TV, cook breakfast, and answer the door without taking a step, and it didn't take long for the luster to wear off our marriage. I had heard the first year of marriage was the best. If the first month of marriage was any indication, I was in for a rude awakening.

Once I went back to work in the Air Force, we only had one car, so Skye was trapped in our little apartment all day. She had no friends, no family, no hobbies. We had no money to do anything anyhow. But what we did have was a TV and Skye watched TV all day while I was gone. This was just at the start of Oprah Winfrey's reign as the queen of daytime television, before she started giving cars away. She talked about many of the problems that went on with housewives. I guess this was good for housewives but it was horrible for husbands who had housewives with nothing else to do but watch *Oprah*. Each night, Skye and I magically had whatever problem Oprah had discussed on her show that day. If the show was about husbands not helping out enough around the house, Skye would yell at me for not helping out enough around the house. If the show was about husbands not showing enough love to their wives, I suddenly didn't show enough love to Skye. One episode was about husbands not helping out enough with the kids. Guess what? Skye and I had the same problem. But wait—we didn't have kids. I was still in trouble, though, because Skye knew that if we did have kids, I wouldn't be helping out enough. I couldn't win.

I felt like I had made a huge mistake. Marriage was supposed to be magical. I started to pray. Up until then, I had not prayed consistently unless there was something that I really needed. But I was at my wits' end with this marriage and with Skye. It had only been a few months and I was already more miserable than I could remember being in the past few years. It was like Skye had turned into a totally different person after we'd said, "I do."

I started to pray that something would change. I prayed that we would figure out how to get along. I prayed if that wasn't possible, we could get an annulment and move on. And finally, I prayed that if none of that happened, maybe I would get hit by a bus and be put out of my misery. I prayed harder than I had ever prayed before for *something* to happen. But why would any of my prayers ever be answered? I'd done nothing for God. Why would he do anything for me? Then one day, I came home from work and opened the door to our small apartment. Sitting on the couch were two young men in white shirts with badges.

Skye sat next to them with a big smile on her face. I did a double take. It wasn't because of the strange men but rather, Skye's huge smile. Whatever these boys were selling I was buying. I hadn't seen Skye smile like that in over a month. They weren't selling anything. They were missionaries from the Church of Jesus Christ of Latter-Day Saints, the church Skye grew up in. It was like the Jehovah's Witness ladies all over again. Except Skye wasn't Gram and it was too late to hide behind a couch.

I walked into the living room and sat down as the two men tried to talk religion. I pretended to listen and was shocked that Skye seemed so interested. Her family was Mormon. She had known this religion her whole life——and had run away from it. Now she was smiling, almost giddy. After the first discussion, they asked me if they could come back and teach us further lessons about their church. Before I could chime in, Skye said, "Absolutely."

That night, Skye and I got along much better than we had in weeks. She was in a better mood and I did not want to upset her by sharing my true feelings about the religious guys. When they returned a few nights later, I politely let them in and got ready to pretend to listen again. This went on for about two months with weekly visits. My heart began to soften as they taught me about their church and about their values and their standards. I began to see what good young men they were, only a little younger than I was. I also saw what it did for Skye and me and our relationship. We started to read the Scriptures together and pray together.

I was not hostile towards them as I was in the first few meetings. I believed in God, but I also believed that I didn't need any organized religion in order to be a good person. But the young men asked me to pray with an open heart. They asked me if I would join their church. At this point, these men had become my friends. I said I'd pray about it. I knew what the answer was going to be before I said it. As nice as these boys were, and as admirable as the standards and values that they taught us had been, there was no way that their church was for me.

I didn't pray that day or the next day, but then I decided that I would do what I said I was going to do, that I would sincerely pray and ask if what these boys were teaching me was true and if I should join their church. I went into our bedroom, kneeled on the box springs and mattress that were on the floor with my knees in the bedroom and my feet in the bathroom. I sincerely prayed with all of my heart for the first time in my life. I don't remember how long that prayer was but it was longer than a few minutes. I don't remember what I said or what questions I asked, but I do remember the answer I received. When I got up off my knees, I knew without a doubt that what those boys had been teaching me was true and that God wanted me to join their church.

That decision to join their church has been one of the biggest decisions in my life. I would not be where I am right now without it. People say a lot of things about organized religion. It may or may not be for you, but without it, I know I would not have had a fraction of the success both personally and professionally that I have had. It has given me the standards and the values to live my life, raise my family, and steer my marriage by. All things that I was missing, since I grew up in a house with uninspiring values or standards.

I know there are people reading this book who are looking for a couch to hide behind as I bring this up but I hope not too many people put the book down. I am not pushing my religion on anybody and this book is not meant to advance my faith or to try to convert anybody to any particular religion. The decision to invite organized religion into my life has changed me for the good, and I had to share.

I also needed all the help I could get from up above.

Chapter 26

A or B?

"Good, better, best. Never let it rest. Until your good is better and your better is best."

— **Tim Duncan**

No matter how much I stared at the TV screen, it seemed to say the same thing every night: "Day Care Employee Charged with Child Molestation." When I looked at my computer screen, all I saw was emails laced with bad news dealing with the real estate industry. It was about this time in my life that things started to get blurry. Granted, things in the world were crazy. But I am talking about things literally getting blurry. My eyesight was going. I could see fine when I was looking at my computer screen but whenever I looked off into the distance, everything seemed to blur together. I dealt with this until I started to get headaches, and then I thought I'd better go see an eye doctor.

The optometrist sat me in his chair and put this alien-looking tool up to my face. We all know this tool. It is the one with seven or eight different lenses on each side. It is called a phoropter and doctors use it to determine a prescription for corrective lenses. This piece of equipment is very subjective: The patient tells the doctor what they see through the lenses. A or B? They switch the lens after you answer and ask again. A? Or B? If you've ever had this test, you know that the more times he asks the question, the harder it gets to answer because the difference is ever so slight.

It is important to note that the optometrist is depending on the patient to tell them what they see. As the doctor goes through the task and flips from one lens to another, we must answer properly if we want to see clearly. Typically, we are only able to see clearly after we have answered the question at least a dozen times.

We can use this technique as we examine the things that happen to us in our lives. Many times, we are in a hurry to give a particular event some sort of meaning that we don't take the time to ask ourselves a few questions before we determine what that meaning is. We fail to look at the situation through different lenses.

Before I am quick to assign a negative meaning to an event, I ask myself a series of questions. How did my actions cause this event to happen? If one of my businesses is not doing as well as it should be, is there something that I could have done or didn't do that caused this? If there are any issues with my health, is there anything that I did or didn't do that could've changed the situation? These types of questions help me take ownership of the situation. And when I take ownership of the problem, that helps me to solve it. Without this ownership, we tend to assign our problems in life to other people and or events.

For example, if the economy is bad and we are struggling financially, we blame our misfortune on the economy. If that's the case, there is nothing that we can do personally because our misfortunes are not our own fault; they are the economy's fault and we cannot control the economy. Or if we are struggling in certain relationships, we blame those struggles on other people. We blame them for what they said or what they did or didn't do. Again, if it is their fault, there is nothing that we can do because it is their problem: the reason that we are having issues is because of what *they* did or didn't do.

This takes all the control away from us and then we are left to wait for circumstances to change or for people to change. We have given away ownership of the problem. I'm sure we've all been in situations where things outside of our control have contributed to some of the situations we did not want to be in. I find that in most cases, there is almost always something I could've done differently that would have changed or even prevented the situation in the first place.

The second part of this strategy is the fact that we sometimes are in situations we cannot control or didn't contribute to. Being able to determine what I can and can't have control of helps me deal with the circumstances of my birth and everything surrounding it. For instance, it was impossible for me to take ownership of the circumstances of my birth. I wasn't there when I was conceived or when my grandfather did those horrible things. There was nothing I could do to change those events, and there was nothing I could do to change people's prejudices against me and my family.

So we ask a different series of questions. How can I use this situation, these events, to strengthen me? I cannot control the winds but I can control how I set my sail. I get to control where this event, or these "winds," take me. What can I learn in this situation?

Sometimes those lessons aren't just for me but they're for the people around me. This was the case on Dawson's first day of eighth grade. Until then, Dawson had been going to a private tutor for homeschooling. We had hired the teacher to work with him one-on-one in hopes that we could accelerate his learning. Dawson was born with FG Syndrome, a rare genetic syndrome that can cause developmental delays. This syndrome caused Dawson to struggle with nearly every subject in school. He couldn't read, write, or do math problems at his age level.

Skye and I decided to reenroll Dawson in the local school so that he could work on his social skills and receive all the services that the school system could provide for children with learning disabilities. But we were apprehensive about Dawson going to public school.

When you look at Dawson, it's not obvious he has a disability. He is a very handsome young man with a great smile and dimples that melt everybody's heart. However, because of that, people also expect him to act the same way that most children his age act.

During the first hour of his first day at school, Dawson sat next to a child who had challenges controlling his anger and emotions. I'm not exactly sure of all the details that led up to this situation but Dawson was carrying on a conversation with this boy and this boy did not want to talk anymore. Dawson did not pick up on that so he kept talking. And believe me, Dawson can talk, and talk, and talk.

The other student became unsettled. He grabbed Dawson around the neck and began to strangle him. Eventually, the teachers were able to pull this other young man off Dawson and restrain him. Dawson was traumatized by this event and did not want to go back to school, ever.

My first reaction before I knew that this child had issues of his own was to go and kick the kid in the butt and give him a piece of my mind. But this story isn't about me, or even about Dawson. Rather, it's about his younger brother, Branson. Branson is the cool kid in our house. He is athletic, handsome, smart, and gregarious. But Branson is still a brother, and as is the case with many brotherly relationships, he gave Dawson a hard time, especially when Dawson did something that was irritating or "abnormal." He had very little patience for some of the things Dawson did or said, even though he knew Dawson had a disability.

But when Branson heard about what had happened to Dawson on his first day at school, he was furious. Branson wanted to go to that school and do the same thing to that kid that the kid had done to Dawson.

"How could they do that to Dawson? They don't know he can't help it," Branson said.

And then he had an "aha" moment. When he saw somebody else treating his brother poorly because of something that he could not control, Branson was furious. But it made him realize that he had not been as patient or understanding as he could have been with Dawson. This situation opened his eyes, giving him a glimpse into what his brother went through on a daily basis.

From that day on, Branson has looked at Dawson differently—kindlier, with more understanding and more compassion. They still disagree sometimes and scream at each other on occasion, as brothers do, but Branson began to understand Dawson that day.

Some of the things in our lives are not necessarily going to be there for our sole purpose. As much as I hated seeing Dawson experience what he did, it changed his relationship with Branson for the better. It even carried over to our youngest son, Grayson, and influenced how he treats Dawson. Because of these discoveries, I decided to give Dawson's first day of eighth grade a positive impact as opposed to a negative one.

I am not suggesting that you live in a Pollyanna world, always wearing rose-colored glasses. But I am suggesting that you take a step back and ask yourself a few A or B questions whenever something happens so you can get a clear vision of exactly what the events mean to you.

Since you are in control of assigning a meaning to everything that happens to you, why on earth would you ever assign something a negative meaning? Using this technique will change your outlook on life and many of its situations. Whenever I struggle to put a positive spin on the situation, I envision that I had two pills, one in each hand. I have a bitter pill in my left hand and I have a better pill in my right hand and I get to choose which one to take. We can be bitter or we can be better. We have the choice. Knowing that we have a choice is a critical part of achieving a better outcome. That control allows us to know it's not our circumstances that define us, it's our choices.

I knew the way I looked at these most recent events could change everything—my career, my businesses, my wife and family, and even the world as a whole. I didn't want to be bitter. I wanted to be better. I needed to be better, not just for me, but for all those people who depended on me: my employees, my wife and kids, and even the world.

I knew I had a story to tell that would help lots of people, other people born into the Unlucky Sperm Club. I just had to make it out of this situation so that my story had a happy ending.

Chapter 27

Ask Better Questions

"Knowledge is having the right answer. Intelligence is asking the right question."

— **Unknown**

For seven months after I saw the horrifying report that one of my day care directors had been accused of child molestation, I suffered setbacks in every area of my life. My businesses were struggling, my marriage had been on life support, and I was failing at being the type of father I wanted to be. My commercial real estate career was nonexistent. Most of the shopping centers I had worked on for the past decade were waiting to be foreclosed. These banks didn't want to do any new leases so they didn't hire any agents. But something began to change in the real estate market. The banks started to sell the properties that they foreclosed. And in order to sell these properties, they needed agents to sell them. This was something that I knew how to do.

I didn't need to *learn* how to sell a shopping center, I was already one of the best in the country at selling and leasing retail real estate. I just needed to get a listing from one of the banks. The trouble was that everyone who was still in commercial real estate wanted the same few listings. To complicate things, the bankers who were now in charge of these properties had been transferred from other divisions within the bank.

They had no experience in selling real estate. They didn't know what to look for in a good agent. You could liken them to me, when I was hiring my Doggie District staff out of Craigslist. Listings were going to brokers who were nowhere near the best in town. The employees at the bank were overworked and had no experience so they hired the person with the biggest smile.

I began to call as many of these bank employees as I could, trying to get an opportunity to list some of their properties. It was like I was working for Michael Kammerling all over again, cold-calling nonstop eight hours a day, getting no after no from the bankers. After weeks of calling every bank I could get the number for, I finally got someone who needed a broker to list a property. She asked me to send my resume and a few transactions I had recently closed. The resume was not a problem but I hadn't closed any sizable deals in over a year. I hoped in light of the economy, she would understand. She did, and she told me that I made the short list of brokers to list the property. Hallelujah!

The listing was for a shopping center that was worth $4 million. A fee from that center would help me get back on my feet again. I prepared a listing presentation for the next 10 days, putting more time and effort in to this one listing pitch than I had for a long time. My assistant, Scott Price, worked 10-hour days alongside me to get the package perfect.

The day of the presentation came and me and my partner, Mike Zobrist, presented to the banker. It went great, and I thought that the listing was in the bag. And then I called the banker two days later to discover the verdict. She had given the listing to another broker. I knew that if we got the listing, we would have done a great job for the bank. I was desperate. I wanted to yell and scream and tell the banker how badly I needed this but I didn't do that. I did the exact opposite.

I took a deep breath and told her that she had made a good choice with the broker she had picked and that he would do a great job on that property for the bank. Then I asked her a question, a question that would make all the difference in the world, although I didn't know it at the time.

"How could I have done a better job at the presentation and been selected as the broker you picked for the listing?"

When I asked that question, I was sincere. I was about as humble as I had ever been in my adult life, and I knew I needed to be better.

She told me it wasn't anything I hadn't done but that the other broker had the listing on that particular property before the bank foreclosed on it. She thought the familiarity would be a huge benefit. I thanked her for the opportunity and hung up the phone. I continued my cold-calling efforts for two more weeks until someone called me. It was the banker who hadn't hired me.

She started out by telling me that she had been very impressed with me and my team at the last presentation. She'd been even more impressed that I was willing to ask her advice on how to do better the next time. She said she was looking for someone like that to work with. Because I'd been willing to ask that question, she gave me a listing to sell one of their properties. I was blown away. I hadn't expected to hear from her again, let alone receive an offer. I almost fell to my knees. The listing was for a $40 million center that was part of one of the nicest shopping centers in Las Vegas. The property also had 50 acres of land that needed to be sold. It was the biggest listing I had ever gotten.

I worked on that shopping center for the next year, selling it off in pieces and finally selling the land to an apartment developer. Those fees earned me the money to keep my businesses going for another year. Throughout that year, not only did I start to sell commercial real estate again but the economy started to improve and people started to do the things they did before the financial meltdown. As time went by, more banks were listing their foreclosed-upon properties to be sold—and because I had sold that massive $40-million center, I got an invite to almost every listing presentation.

Doggie District was also beginning to gain momentum again under Austin's leadership. All the resorts were heading in the right direction and most were cash flow positive.

As good as things were looking, I still had two things that kept me up at night. What would happen with Bright Child as the investigation of the child molester dragged on? And what would happen between me and Skye? We were both still trying to make it work but we often fought. Some days were wonderful and other days had us thinking that no matter how much we wanted it to work, our family might just fall apart. I had to look for the positive. Lots of things were going in the right direction, and I could gain inspiration from the things that were going well.

It was true that things were looking better but the truth is not always what you think it is.

Chapter 28

Who's Your Daddy?

"The truth will set you free. But first it will make you miserable."

— **James A. Garfield**

Over the next few months, I was deposed three times by the different attorneys—the state's, the alleged child molester's, and mine. I got asked the same question dozens of different ways. They would ask ridiculous questions, like did I know my director was a pedophile before I hired him? Did I ever witness him harming a child? Did I cover up the fact that he was molesting children? These questions got so absurd that I actually burst out in frustration in front of one of the attorneys.

"Why are you asking me these ridiculous questions? Do you really think that I knew he was a child molester when I hired him? Do you think if I had witnessed him hurting a child, I wouldn't beat him to a pulp and call the police? What are you guys trying to accomplish by asking these types of questions?" I yelled.

"We're just trying to get to the truth," the attorney said. I wanted the truth as well. I wanted this all to be over. But I knew the truth could hurt. I had learned early on to brace for the pain.

There was a girl I really liked in middle school. Her name was Lori. I had a crush on her for a few months. She was a cheerleader and I was on the recreational football team. One day, I went to her house on my three-wheeler. As I drove down her dirt road, my mind was full of all the middle-school-love feelings one experiences. I had a girlfriend. I was the football player. She was the cheerleader. Life was good.

Lori's dad came home and walked out back where we were riding my three-wheeler around her back yard.

"Who's this, Lori?" her dad asked politely as he looked at me.

"This is Nelson Tressler. He's my friend," Lori said innocently.

"Oh," he said. His demeanor changed and he walked into the house through the sliding glass door, not bothering to close it.

"Lori, come here," he said sternly.

She went over to talk to him, but he still used a voice that I was sure most of their neighbors heard. He said, "Do you know who that kid is? That's Nelson Tressler. You are not to see him again." He then mumbled something I couldn't hear.

After a few awkward minutes, Lori stepped back through the sliding glass door. She was sure to close it. She looked pale. Her eyes had tears in them.

"My dad says I can't see you anymore. You have to leave now," Lori said, her voice trembling.

"Uh, why?" I asked. Even though I'd heard her dad, I think I still was hoping it had something to do with me having arrived there without an adult being home.

"My dad just told me that your grandfather shot my grandfather."

I felt all the air whoosh out of my body. It felt like I was floating in the air, stuck in a dream—no, a nightmare. There was no way this was true, was it?

"I'm, I'm sorry," was all I could say before I turned to get my three-wheeler to head home.

My grandfather had wounded her grandfather that day. It wasn't the police officer he killed but the other officer he critically wounded during his rampage. I felt so stupid. There were times in my life that I forgot who I was and what I represented. Days where I almost felt normal. Days where I was the football player dating the cheerleader. But those days always ended with days like this one. Days when the reality of who I was would come and sucker punch me right between the eyes. I cried the entire way home. It wasn't fair. I didn't do any of those horrible things. I wasn't even born when Pap shot those officers. Why was I paying the price of his terrible deeds? When I got home, I went to find my mom. It was time to have a talk. She could tell I had been crying.

"What's wrong?" she asked, with concern in her voice. I explained to her what had transpired and the unfairness of it all. I was angry and hurt and deflated with life.

Tears started to come to her eyes. "Nelson, I have to tell you something. It's hard for me to say and you can never tell anyone I told you. Nelson, your father is not Ronald Seymore, the cop that Pap shot."

"What?" I asked.

"He is not your dad. I had to lie about that to save your pap's life. He would have been put to death if I didn't tell the jury that story about Seymore raping me and me getting pregnant with you. I did it to save my dad's life, and I'm sorry I did it. I am sorry for you and for what it put you through. But I was 16 years old and everyone was telling me that it was the only way Pap was not going to be put to death. They told me if the jury knew that Pap's only reason for killing Seymore was because they shut down his garbage dump, he would for sure get the death penalty. It was his only chance and I was the only one that could save him. I was just trying to save my dad's life and not thinking of what it meant for me or you in the future. If I knew what the future held for you, I would have never done it. I am sorry."

I couldn't believe what she was saying. What was she talking about, that Officer Seymore wasn't my father? If he wasn't, then who was? And where was he and why didn't he want to be in my life? I wanted to stay angry and even hate my mom for what she was telling me. But then she said it again, and I knew she had never meant it more. She kept on saying it, between sobbing, "I'm sorry, Nelson"

She cried uncontrollably. Up to that point, I had only seen my mom cry at Jim's abusive hands, and although it had hurt me to see her in pain from the beatings she endured, I could tell that this was the most pain my mom had ever experienced. I tried to put my own confusion aside and reached out to hold her. She continued to cry for what seemed like an hour, sporadically catching her breath and then convulsing again into her weeping and groaning. I kept on holding her, trying to console her, and telling her that it was okay. I told her I didn't blame her for what she had done, but it was clear that she blamed herself.

After my mom caught her breath and stopped crying, she said, "Your dad is Buck Shawley."

I knew Buck. We lived next to him for a while at one of our houses. He had three young kids. I would still see him once in a while when he came to Coleville looking to buy a junk part from my Uncle Bub. In fact, I remember playing football on the street one day when he drove up and asked me if I knew where Bub was. I told him I thought he was up at the junk yard. He thanked me and then took out his wallet and gave me a dollar bill. I thanked him. And he got in his car and drove away. I'd never thought twice about that experience until now. I was just happy to have some money to buy a soda that day. I can't remember if that was the last time I saw him or not.

A year earlier, Buck was driving drunk and crashed, killing him and the passengers in his car. I remember hearing about the crash and feeling bad for the people but that was it.

Drunk driving had taken the lives of both my stepfather and my biological father.

The conversation eventually ended, leaving my life in pretty much the same way it was before. I knew the truth. I couldn't tell anyone the truth about the rape that didn't happen. My grandfather was still fighting to have his sentence reduced. I now knew who my biological father was, but he was dead and apparently, he had fathered eight or nine other children along the way, so I was without a dad but now had more brothers and sisters.

But a weight had been lifted off me that day. I wasn't the product of a violent rape. I wasn't a child who was here because of a horrifying situation. Every time my mom looked at me, she wasn't thinking of that awful night when she was 15 years old and raped. I can't explain how that knowledge freed me. It didn't matter that I couldn't tell anyone else, I knew who I was for the first time in my life.

The truth was liberating.

Chapter 29

Tender Mercies

"The Tender Mercies of the Lord are real, and they do not occur randomly or merely by coincidence."

— David A Bednar

After months of investigations, a small glimmer of light appeared at the end of my dark tunnel of a life. It was a family friend of the child molester's who had made the initial allegation against him. The family friend's two daughters accused him of molesting them on multiple occasions, including at the old day care where he worked before Bright Child. But there was no evidence that abuse took place in my centers. He had never touched a Bright Child Learning Center kid and the tie between my day cares and his sins began to fray. The media lost interest, as he was now just another sick individual messing with family friends instead of a monster who ran a childcare center in Las Vegas.

The guilt that I had felt after seeing my day care director on the news a year earlier evaporated. I hadn't been the cause of any child getting abused. I felt horrible for the two girls he did abuse and hoped that he would pay dearly for his crimes, but the weight that came off of my shoulders when I found out that no child under my watch had been abused was invigorating.

We were not going to have to shut down. We could manage with limited enrollments and try to build them back up. Parents would not blame me for my decision, and people almost started looking me in the eye again. Don't get me wrong, it's not like one day everything went back to normal. The damage was done. But the economy was rebounding and things were starting to look like they would work out for the businesses.

There was even hope for Skye and me. Earlier that year, I had moved back in, although I slept on the couch most nights. We were still able for the most part to keep our troubles secret from our kids. At least we were civil to each other. Through counseling, we both realized that we loved each other and that our marriage was the most important thing in each of our lives. Knowing was one thing but being able to move past the fights and the unkind words was something totally different.

Skye and I struggled to get along when it was just our family so we tried to invite other families on our outings. It made the entire experience better for her and me. The Nishes were our go-to family. They had three kids the same ages as Dawson and Branson. The kids would entertain each other and we adults could have some free time. We loved going to Duck Creek, Utah, together. Duck Creek is three hours north of Las Vegas, located in the Wasatch mountains at 9,000 feet of elevation. When it was 114 degrees in Las Vegas, it was 75 degrees at Duck Creek. We spent nearly every weekend one summer there with the Nishes.

Casey Nish was a cancer survivor. Not only was he a survivor, he'd actually been given his last rites three years earlier while fighting leukemia. The doctors told his wife, Lanny, to have the family come and say goodbye. They didn't think Casey would last the night. The Nishes had already been through the hell of losing a child in an accident a year earlier when one of their sons was run over by a car in front of their house. Lanny brought their three kids into the room to say goodbye to their father.

Casey didn't die that night or the night after. The doctors threw around the word "miracle" a lot the next few days. Days turned into weeks, and eventually Casey was released from the hospital, free of any of the cancer that had his family just weeks earlier saying goodbye to him.

Although Casey was cancer-free, he knew it could come back without warning. He believed he had been given the gift of time. It was never lost on me how Casey cherished every moment with his wife and kids. Casey had a habit of walking over to one of his kids no matter what the circumstance or time of day, just whenever he felt like it, to give them a hug or tickle their back. He understood what a gift it was to be with his family, and he was not going to waste a minute of it.

This reverence for time with family was not lost on me and Skye that summer we spent with them at Duck Creek. Through Casey, we saw how truly important family was and what a gift we had right in front of us. Casey helped us to realize that we could get through these hard times and that the effort to get through them would be worth it.

Skye and I got along best when we were with the Nishes in Duck Creek. Those good times started to follow us home and we began to remember why we first fell in love. We also realized how truly blessed we were. Regardless of what happened with the businesses or the economy, we realized that our most precious treasure was our family and as long as we had our family, we had everything.

That became even more clear when Casey's cancer returned. The doctors again told Lanny to have his family come say goodbye. This time Casey passed. I believe Casey being spared that first time was a true miracle. Like Casey, I also believe he had been given the gift of more time with his children. Those extra four years with his young children made all the difference when it came to them getting to know their father and learning from him.

But I also think it was a miracle for my family. Because of that, Skye and I changed a lot of the things we did. We no longer took each other for granted. We tried to always have patience with each other. I quit focusing on the unrealistic expectations I had for her and focused instead on how much appreciation I genuinely had for her. Our relationship transformed as I started to see all of the qualities that made Skye so wonderful. We started to have good day after good day, and the momentum quickly had us more in love then we'd ever been. If we ever forgot how blessed we were, we would pause and remember that Casey would have given anything to have what we have.

Casey also taught me an important lesson when it comes to how we value our time. Time is by far our most precious resource. It should never be wasted or taken for granted. Every day we have is indeed a blessing, and we should use each day to its fullest because we never know how long we have on this earth. I used to think I would do things later—tomorrow, next week, or next year. Casey helped me to realize that tomorrow may never come. Do it today, especially when it comes to your family.

Just a few months earlier, I couldn't wait for each day to be over. I now found myself trying to stretch as much out of each day as I can. A quote that sums this concept up is, "The days are long, but the years are short." I know it doesn't feel that way when you are having a bad day, but believe me—that is one of the truest statements you will ever hear.

Chapter 30

IGOTSMARTER

"Helping one person might not change the world, but it will change the world for one person."

— Unknown

Over a decade has passed since the crash of 2008 and the subsequent turmoil it caused not only me and my family but the entire world. The economy eventually not only turned around, it became better than it ever had been. My father-in-law and I not only saved the day care centers, we were able to sell them for a healthy profit. The buyer is still operating them and doing very well. She's grown the business to nine locations in the Las Vegas Valley. What a blessing it was to be able to sell them when we did. Due to my father-in-law's kidney trouble, he had to retire early from his dental practice. He was fortunate enough to receive a kidney transplant soon after. He is doing well and enjoying his retirement.

Austin thrived running Doggie District Pet Resort. He helped to grow it into one of the largest privately held pet resort chains in America before we sold it for more money than either of us ever thought possible. Doggie District is still going strong, and Austin has moved on to bigger and better things.

Skye and I are about to celebrate our 25th wedding anniversary. It flew by. It feels like it's only been five minutes … under water. (Skye doesn't like that joke either.) But in all seriousness, I couldn't be happier. We are best friends and are raising three awesome young men together.

Dawson is now 22. He graduated high school, and in the tradition of our church and community, served a full-time mission for his church on a ranch that raises cattle to provide meat to those in need. He moved away from home and lived with another missionary for a year while they served on the cattle ranch. Dawson had to cook his own meals, wash his own clothes, and even clean his own room. Not only didn't Dawson get paid for his service, he had to pay his own expenses during his year of service. It was hard for him, mainly because he is so social. The ranch was 35 miles away from the nearest town. You have to take a road that is literally called "the loneliest road in America" to get to the ranch. But he stuck it out, finished his year, and provided great service for the people who would benefit from the beef he helped raise. He loves working with his hands and is now working a construction maintenance job when he's not riding his horse, Joker.

Branson is 17 and graduating this year. He has received a Division I scholarship to Dixie State University to play baseball. He has decided to put that scholarship on hold for two years while he serves a mission for our church.

Grayson is 14 and in eighth grade. He is by far the smartest person in our family. One of my lasting arguments with Skye is where he gets his brains from. She thinks it's from her side of the family; I think we got the wrong baby back from the hospital. He is a great baseball player and has been named the captain of the volleyball team this year. He's the best negotiator in our house and has built up quite the pin collection through his superior trading skills.

As the banks continued to sell off their foreclosures, my commercial real estate career found new life. I again was the number-one retail broker nationwide and I'm still part of the number-one team locally 20 years in a row. I have since taken a break from commercial real estate to pursue yet another business venture.

It's the business that I was placed on this earth to start.

Since 2000, when I graduated college, I have been obsessed with personal development and goals. I'd spend every New Year's Day writing my goals and planning for the future. I'd reflect on the previous year, seeing what worked and what didn't, and then write down my goals for the coming New Year. My obsession for goal achievement started with that first big goal of being the first Tressler to get a college degree. That obsession fed my need to find personal development programs and seminars. I went to every one I could afford. The more I did it, the more I used what I learned, the more success I had. It didn't stop at seminars and classes; I consumed any book or magazine that was on goals and personal development.

What I learned is that achieving your life's biggest goals is not left up to happenstance. Not only can anyone set a goal and work to achieve it but if you have enough time, focus, and energy you can accomplish any goal you set your mind to. That fact was further cemented in my mind by this fact: if someone like me, a full-fledged member of the Unlucky Sperm Club, can have success through personal development and goals, then anyone can.

As I got on the other side of the chaos, I was asked to give speeches on the topics of personal development and goals. I became known as the "Goal Guy" in my circle of friends. Friends and colleagues would ask me to help them with their goals. I love everything about goals and knew the power of goals, so I was more than happy to help people come up with a plan to reach their own goals. Sometimes I'd spend three to four hours with individuals, teaching them all of my philosophies, strategies, and techniques. A week or two later, I'd check in and ask how it was going.

"I need to get on that," they'd say.

It was like a kick in the gut. I spent so much time and effort creating a road map with them and they hadn't even put forth the effort to put gas in the car yet. Come on! At first, I was upset, but then I realized people struggled with the implementation of their goal plan. I realized the key is that *other* people need to know about these goals and to be vested with them. The people who are struggling needed someone to help them be accountable to themselves. They needed a partner who would help them strive for a higher standard, someone else whose expectations are on the line.

I saw a need I could address, a role I could fill. I offered to become a success partner for a friend. I wasn't there to "hold him accountable" in the typical sense. These were his goals and dreams, not mine. He had no accountability to me. I was there to help him be successful in achieving his goals. I was there to help him be accountable to himself.

The results once I took on this role were amazing. My partner started to do the things he said he was going to do. Not only did he do a better job of doing what he knew he needed to do but I, too, did a better job on my goals. I knew he was aware of my personal goals and what I said I'd do to fulfill them. It was as if we had cracked the code to goal fulfillment. Before I knew it, I was a success partner for three people. The results were the same for all three people. They did a much better job sticking to their goals when they had a success partner.

I had an epiphany. Let's group together, I told them. Help each other and rotate success partners.

I invited a few more guys I had also previously talked to about goals with to join the group and we started holding meetings and helping each other on our roads to success. It was truly amazing to see the group members' transformations. They were all great guys before the group but now they were living life with purpose. They were all reaching an even higher level of success in every area of their lives. I really knew I was on to something when I would see one of the men's wives from the group out shopping or at church. They would tell me, "You can never stop having your group. My husband is a different man. He is more thoughtful, more active, healthier, more everything. Don't you ever stop that group."

The participants' wives were reaping the benefits of their partners' goal setting. So much so that all the wives started their own group because of the results they saw. These groups were helping people live happier, more productive lives.

It was the "aha!" moment I never knew I needed. At that moment, I realized why I was born into the Unlucky Sperm Club. This right here is what I was put on this earth to do. This is a job that would change people's lives. Not just their immediate lives but their ensuing generations' lives. If I had never gone to college and joined the Air Force, my kids might not have the life they have today. One small change in an individual's life can impact the generations to follow.

For example, look at my family situation in Bellefonte and my family now, in Las Vegas. Polar opposites. My grandfather was in prison serving life without the possibility of parole when he was 48 years old. I'm helping people tackle their biggest life goals at the age of 48. My mom had me, no education, no husband, and little hope of a bright future at 17. My 17-year-old son is preparing to serve a full-time mission for his church, with a scholarship to a Division I school. This total transformation took place in one generation and was set in motion by just one goal. This is the power of goals.

With everything I have gone through in my life, I have finally decided I wanted to spend the rest of it serving others. It isn't about me anymore but what I can do to impact others' lives through personal development. When I get to the end of my life, if I've been able to do that for one person, it will be worth it. My goal is to help millions. But if I can know I've helped one, that will be enough.

So I've taken every lesson I learned from the dead-end street to the collapse of the economy to making it out on the other side and created a program called IGOTSMARTER. That program provides all the tools, knowledge, and support people need to achieve their biggest goals in life. IGOTSMARTER is so much more than a group of people striving to help each other achieve their goals. We have developed a state-of-the-art app and website that helps people through the goal-achievement program that is IGOTSMARTER. It's a community of people that want to reach their potential and to achieve their goals. IGOTSMARTER helps its members become better versions of themselves through its tools and collective knowledge and most importantly, the support that it provides its members.

We all have that potential in us. We just have to take those steps and make those choices to get us where we're destined to be.

After selling my businesses and retiring from being a commercial real estate agent, I now have enough passive income to provide for me and my family for the rest of my life. I have a great marriage and my three boys are on their way to becoming great men. In large part, I owe all of these accomplishments to my ability to set and achieve goals in my life.

This is my time to go back to the bucket and show the other crabs what is out there. This is my time to show people what is possible and what type of potential lives inside of them. This is my time to show people that you don't have to play the hand that you were dealt and that there are four-letter F-words that can propel you to your dreams and your goals. It's my time to show people that we are what we choose to be and that we need to feed the good wolf that lives inside of us. It's my time to help people clear the static from their lives so that they can focus on the things that are important to them and to help people realize that every choice they make is a trade. The more good trades we make, the more fulfilled we will be.

It's my time to show the people who have been discriminated against that it doesn't matter what name or number is on your jersey; it matters what's in your heart. It's my time to help people forgive and lighten their burdens, and to show people that things don't have to be the way that they are, that we control the sails of our own ship no matter which way the wind blows. It is my time to fulfill my purpose for being put on this earth under the circumstances I was placed in.

It is my time, but it is also your time.

The IGOTSMARTER program is filled with the strategies I have used throughout my life to not only overcome tough situations but to excel in spite of those situations. This program combines the best philosophies and strategies that I've used throughout my life to accomplish my biggest goals. They have helped me come from being born in very trying circumstances to living a life I couldn't have even imagined 30 years ago. And

I am confident that if you follow the strategies and philosophies in this program that you will also be able to become a member of the "Unlucky Sperm Club."

I want you to think back on the last New Year's resolution you set. Go ahead, think about it. Chances are, you've already failed or forgotten about the resolution you made, even if you're reading this at the end of January. Don't feel bad. About 92 percent of New Year's resolutions fail within the first 15 days. That's right, come January 15th or so, 92 percent of the New Year's resolutions made around the world have already failed. There are lots of reasons for this but this does not have to be the case.

How different would your life be if you were able to achieve your New Year's resolutions or any goal for that matter? How different would the world be if more people were able to accomplish their life's biggest goals? How different would the future of the world be if people could accomplish their life's biggest goals?

What if Bill Gates hadn't followed through with his goal of having a personal computer on every desk in the US? How different would your life be if Steve Jobs hadn't followed through with his goal of building Apple computers and then the iPod, iPhone, and iPad? How different would your life be if Henry Ford had quit on his dreams of every family having a car? This list could go on forever, every great invention, discovery, or event started first with a goal.

Now imagine how different our lives would be if a person we've never heard of didn't give up on their goal. We don't know what that incredible discovery, invention, or event was because they never followed through and lost focus. Who knows, maybe they would have developed something that could change our lives even more than Bill Gates, Steve Jobs, or Henry Ford. And what if that person was you?

Using the IGOTSMARTER program can help you change the world. However, I developed IGOTSMARTER so people could change *their* worlds by achieving the goals that are most important to them. And together we can change the entire world one person, and one goal, at a time.

I don't give fear much place in my life anymore knowing what I know now. I don't even fear a four-foot-tall man with a hook. I've long since stopped running in zigzag lines, looking behind every tree when I am in the woods back in Pennsylvania. But there is one thing that scares me to death when I think about it. It's that if I didn't set and fulfill that first big goal of being the first person in my family to graduate college, I may have forfeited this life I am now living. That everything that I have done since I set and then achieved that goal may have never come to be. It is horrifying to contemplate. It's so frightening to contemplate because I know that I have fallen short on achieving other goals in my life, and I will never know what I forfeited because I was not able to achieve those goals.

Do you remember the bigger and better things that Austin decided to move on to? Well, he has decided to join the IGOTSMARTER team, and together we are determined to spend the rest of our lives helping others to achieve their goals so that they don't have to worry about what life they have forfeited because of unfulfilled goals.

Join us in our efforts to change the world one person and one goal at a time by changing *your* life using the IGOTSMARTER program. Go to IGOTSMARTER.com and join the program that will change your life.

And maybe you will see that being a member of the Unlucky Sperm Club—or having to overcome whatever circumstances you feel are weighing you down—doesn't make you so unlucky after all.

CPSIA information can be obtained
at www.ICGtesting.com
Printed in the USA
FSHW011115241020
75058FS